Magento Extensions Development

Design, build, and maintain a powerful, secure, and complete extension for Magento 2, the world's favorite e-commerce platform

Jérémie Bouchet

BIRMINGHAM - MUMBAI

Magento Extensions Development

First published: June 2016

Production reference: 1270616

Published by Packt Publishing Ltd.
Livery Place
35 Livery Street
Birmingham B3 2PB, UK.

ISBN 978-1-78328-677-5

www.packtpub.com

Credits

Author
Jérémie Bouchet

Reviewer
Ash Isaac

Commissioning Editor
Rubal Kaur

Acquisition Editor
Kirk D'costa

Content Development Editor
Divij Kotian

Technical Editors
Rutuja Vaze

Jayesh Sonawane

Copy Editor
Safis Editing

Project Coordinator
Ritika Manoj

Proofreader
Safis Editing

Indexer
Hemangini Bari

Production Coordinator
Aparna Bhagat

Cover Work
Aparna Bhagat

About the Author

Jérémie Bouchet is a French backend web developer and entrepreneur, who began his career by selling fair music. With his certification (Jérémie obtained the Magento Certified Developer certification in 2012) and his skills and knowledge of each side of the trade, Jérémie has all the keys to make a success of numerous Magento projects, by working on various complex functionalities.

He is a cofounder of Blackbird Agency (`http://black.bird.eu`), a web agency specializing in Magento projects and e-commerce challenges.

He initiated and managed other exciting projects in his city, such as a coworking space designed for web freelancers (`https://quai10.org`) or the `http://whomadethis.site` website, a web service that helps people to know *who made a website*.

I would like to thank my associates and friends Anthony and Benjamin for their support and patience during the whole period I was writing this book, and Ceyhun and Thomas for their help on specific topics. Many thanks to Divij for his encouragement and kindness since the beginning of this adventure.

About the Reviewer

Ash Isaac is a full-stack engineer with over a decade of broad expertise in software development and consulting. He has worked as a system analyst in a large multinational software company, as a solopreneur bootstrapping a Magento-based product, and as a mentor to students engaged in entrepreneurship to benefit the poor. He is currently working on a cloud-based Enterprise SaaS eClinical product.

I dedicate this book to my family Kristy, Vikram, Sareetha, Jay, and Selvan.

---

www.PacktPub.com

eBooks, discount offers, and more

Did you know that Packt offers eBook versions of every book published, with PDF and ePub files available? You can upgrade to the eBook version at www.PacktPub.com and as a print book customer, you are entitled to a discount on the eBook copy. Get in touch with us at customercare@packtpub.com for more details.

At www.PacktPub.com, you can also read a collection of free technical articles, sign up for a range of free newsletters and receive exclusive discounts and offers on Packt books and eBooks.

https://www2.packtpub.com/books/subscription/packtlib

Do you need instant solutions to your IT questions? PacktLib is Packt's online digital book library. Here, you can search, access, and read Packt's entire library of books.

Why subscribe?

- Fully searchable across every book published by Packt
- Copy and paste, print, and bookmark content
- On demand and accessible via a web browser

Table of Contents

Preface

The book will support you in the writing of innovative and complex extensions. Starting at the beginning, this book will cover how to set up a development environment, such as GIT registering and many other development tools, which allows you to be really efficient in your functionality writing. We will then move on to a broad overview of the best practices for scaling your module in a high-load environment. After these foundations, we will see how to use Test-Driven Development (TDD) and unit tests to handle our code. We will build a complex, international-ready extension together step by step. Next, we will see how to protect the final user's data.

Finally, we will see how to publish the extension to the new Magento Connect marketplace and protect your intellectual property.

After reading this book, you will have learned everything you need to become an invaluable extension editor, whether it is for your customers' needs or for your own requirements.

What this book covers

Chapter 1, Introduction to Extension Development, will discuss the need for complex extensions in Magento Marketplace. We will discover that marketable extensions fulfil a complex purpose and begin to write the foundations of our extension.

Chapter 2, Deeper Extension Development, continues to develop our extension and add some backend capabilities.

Chapter 3, Best Practices and Scaling for the Web, covers the creation of a new product type. We will design and study all the techniques used to speed up our code and think about security first.

Chapter 4, Magento and Test-driven Development, will discover TDD and how Magento handles PHPUnit tests in order to guarantee your customers the best extension.

Chapter 5, Internationalization, will talk about how to localize our module's contents and functionalities.

Chapter 6, Optimizing for Speed and Measuring Conversion Rates, will concentrate our efforts on performance: how to measure the speed and resources the code uses and what impact we can have on speed.

Chapter 7, Module Creation Etiquette, covers how to ensure that you will provide the best trustworthy extension in the market.

Chapter 8, Optimization for Teamwork Development, will cover the basics of project sharing and how to speed up development in a small or big team.

Chapter 9, Magento Marketplace, will provide information on how to publish the code on Magento Marketplace and what to know to ensure that your extension will be validated.

What you need for this book

As a Magento developer, you already have a local web server such as Apache or Nginx and a database server such as MySQL. The book will discuss and explain all the other tools you will need for this book.

Who this book is for

If you want to write a specific customization or a large, new, and full-featured extension to Magento 2, this book is intended for you. You must be an intermediate-to-professional-level developer in PHP to appreciate this book.

Conventions

In this book, you will find a number of text styles that distinguish between different kinds of information. Here are some examples of these styles and an explanation of their meaning.

Code words in text, database table names, folder names, filenames, file extensions, pathnames, dummy URLs, user input, and Twitter handles are shown as follows: "Create a `Helper` class of the extension by adding the following code into the `Helper[extension_path]/Helper/Event.php`"

A block of code is set as follows:

```
<?xml version="1.0"?>
<config xmlns:xsi="http://www.w3.org/2001/XMLSchema-instance" xsi:noNa
mespaceSchemaLocation="urn:magento:framework:Module/etc/module.xsd">
<module name="Blackbird_TicketBlaster" setup_version="1.0.0" />
</config>
```

When we wish to draw your attention to a particular part of a code block, the relevant lines or items are set in bold:

```
<router id="standard">
<route id="events" frontName="events">
<module name="Blackbird_TicketBlaster" />
</route>
```

Any command-line input or output is written as follows:

```
php bin/magento module:enable
php bin/magento setup:upgrade
```

New terms and **important words** are shown in bold. Words that you see on the screen, for example, in menus or dialog boxes, appear in the text like this: "Clicking the **Next** button moves you to the next screen."

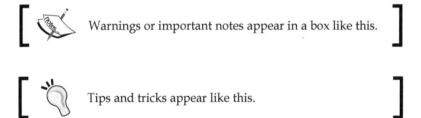

> Warnings or important notes appear in a box like this.

> Tips and tricks appear like this.

Reader feedback

Feedback from our readers is always welcome. Let us know what you think about this book—what you liked or disliked. Reader feedback is important for us as it helps us develop titles that you will really get the most out of.

To send us general feedback, simply e-mail feedback@packtpub.com, and mention the book's title in the subject of your message.

If there is a topic that you have expertise in and you are interested in either writing or contributing to a book, see our author guide at www.packtpub.com/authors.

Customer support

Now that you are the proud owner of a Packt book, we have a number of things to help you to get the most from your purchase.

Downloading the example code

You can clone the repository of the created extension, which is available at `https://bitbucket.org/blackbirdagency/ticket-blaster`.

You can download the example code files for this book from your account at `http://www.packtpub.com`. If you purchased this book elsewhere, you can visit `http://www.packtpub.com/support` and register to have the files e-mailed directly to you.

You can download the code files by following these steps:

1. Log in or register to our website using your e-mail address and password.
2. Hover the mouse pointer on the **SUPPORT** tab at the top.
3. Click on **Code Downloads & Errata**.
4. Enter the name of the book in the **Search** box.
5. Select the book for which you're looking to download the code files.
6. Choose from the drop-down menu where you purchased this book from.
7. Click on **Code Download**.

You can also download the code files by clicking on the **Code Files** button on the book's webpage at the Packt Publishing website. This page can be accessed by entering the book's name in the **Search** box. Please note that you need to be logged in to your Packt account.

Once the file is downloaded, please make sure that you unzip or extract the folder using the latest version of:

- WinRAR / 7-Zip for Windows
- Zipeg / iZip / UnRarX for Mac
- 7-Zip / PeaZip for Linux

The code bundle for the book is also hosted on GitHub at `https://github.com/PacktPublishing/Magento-Extensions-Development`. We also have other code bundles from our rich catalog of books and videos available at `https://github.com/PacktPublishing/`. Check them out!

Downloading the color images of this book

We also provide you with a PDF file that has color images of the screenshots/diagrams used in this book. The color images will help you better understand the changes in the output. You can download this file from `http://www.packtpub.com/sites/default/files/downloads/MagentoExtensionsDevelopment_ColorImages.pdf`.

Errata

Although we have taken every care to ensure the accuracy of our content, mistakes do happen. If you find a mistake in one of our books—maybe a mistake in the text or the code—we would be grateful if you could report this to us. By doing so, you can save other readers from frustration and help us improve subsequent versions of this book. If you find any errata, please report them by visiting `http://www.packtpub.com/submit-errata`, selecting your book, clicking on the **Errata Submission Form** link, and entering the details of your errata. Once your errata are verified, your submission will be accepted and the errata will be uploaded to our website or added to any list of existing errata under the Errata section of that title.

To view the previously submitted errata, go to `https://www.packtpub.com/books/content/support` and enter the name of the book in the search field. The required information will appear under the **Errata** section.

Piracy

Piracy of copyrighted material on the Internet is an ongoing problem across all media. At Packt, we take the protection of our copyright and licenses very seriously. If you come across any illegal copies of our works in any form on the Internet, please provide us with the location address or website name immediately so that we can pursue a remedy.

Please contact us at `copyright@packtpub.com` with a link to the suspected pirated material.

We appreciate your help in protecting our authors and our ability to bring you valuable content.

Questions

If you have a problem with any aspect of this book, you can contact us at `questions@packtpub.com`, and we will do our best to address the problem.

1
Introduction to Extension Development

Before I was a Magento Developer, I sold *fair trade* music from my own e-commerce website. Ten years ago, it was difficult to propose a technically new website to buy and download music from hundreds of artists; so much so that I spent all my time developing this part. There were a lot of other functionalities to develop, such as the customer relationship interface, the artist relationship interface, and much more; I said to myself that they would arrive later.

Later, my society, DiskOverMusic, began to organize concerts; what an exciting new challenge! Concert halls, technicians, lights, drinks, there were thousands of things to do for it. But how could I sell tickets to the millions of fans?.

Now, Magento exists and offers us a fantastic playground to develop everything our clients need in order to make the Internet innovative and secure. Standard development and the Magento framework allow you to develop clean, fast, and secure code to bring new functionalities to the community.

In our very first chapter, we will discuss the need for complex extensions in the Magento Marketplace. We will discover that marketable extensions fulfil a complex purpose.

Thanks to Magento, we will create TicketBlaster, a module which will enable a store owner to sell seated tickets to events at a venue.

Magento is an out of the box e-commerce platform with many features, such as catalog navigation, promotion rules, tax rules, reports, and order management, which enable the store owner to begin to sell his products. However, all this out of the box functionality does not allow him to differentiate his store from others, interface with third party web applications, and offer good quality marketing and social services to the customer, as well as — maybe the most important requirement — providing an answer to the specificities of the profession the store owner needs.

Thus, Magento's community, composed of hundreds of developers and editors, distribute a lot of free and paid complex extensions in the Magento Marketplace. The extensions cover usage in customer experience (gifts, social, and so on), site management (administration, automations, and so on), integrations (payment, shipping, gateways, and so on), marketing (ads, email marketing, SEO, and so on), tech utilities, and themes. We will explore the Marketplace in detail in *Chapter 8. Optimization for Teamwork Development.*

In this chapter, we will cover the following topics:

- Creating an extension
- Registering dependencies with Composer
- Managing our work with **Git** source control

Getting started

This book assumes you have an intermediate knowledge of Magento development and installation. You will see many examples and screenshots of the Magento I use for this book; I use a local web server running with Apache (only) on an Ubuntu desktop OS.

The Magento I use is the latest beta version at the time of writing: Magento 2 C.E. version. 1.0.0-beta. That's why my local server is reachable at the following local address: `http://magento2.local.com/`.

My Magento admin panel is located at `http://magento2.local.com/backoff`.

 One of the first good practices is to use another admin panel URL, other than admin.

Obviously, this installation isn't recommended for a production environment, but can teach you where the main problems can appear with a web server that runs a Magento. And it is perfect for web development, because you are not limited by an Internet connection and you can immediately resolve problems.

> If you are interested in a production server installation, or if you have a development server in your organization, you can find a complete installation script at https://bitbucket.org/jeremie_blackbird/iams.

Creating an extension

When you want to create an extension, the first step is to think about its goal and functionalities. Take this important time to define and draft a prototype of the main functionalities and how they will be managed by the admin. For this step, you can use some tools available on the web, such as Proto.io, Balsamiq, or Moqups; they allow you to create and share prototypes that look and work like your extension should, but without code.

> Visit http://proto.io, http://balsamiq.com, and http://moqups.com to discover these useful tools.

Another step is to look at others extensions, in order to determine whether you are writing an already existing extension, that performs the same function as yours. It doesn't matter, but if this is the case, I recommend you make a better extension than the original!

Finally, open your favourite IDE and continue to read this chapter. Here, we will begin to create TicketBlaster, a module which will enables a store owner to sell seated tickets to events at a venue.

The files that handle our extension

In the following steps, we will create the files necessary to our extension:

1. Create the extension structure by creating the following folder structure:
   - app/code/Blackbird
   - app/code/Blackbird/TicketBlaster
   - app/code/Blackbird/TicketBlaster/etc

2. Register the extension by creating the `module.xml` file in the `app/code/Blackbird/etc` folder and add this content to it:

   ```xml
   <?xml version="1.0"?>
   <config xmlns:xsi="http://www.w3.org/2001/XMLSchema-instance" xsi:noNamespaceSchemaLocation="urn:magento:framework:Module/etc/module.xsd">
   <module name="Blackbird_TicketBlaster" setup_version="1.0.0" />
   </config>
   ```

   This code informs Magento that a module named TicketBlaster with the namespace `Blackbird`, located in the `app/code/Blackbird` folder can be loaded and activated.

   > `Blackbird` is the namespace of the module; it will be visible to developers and integrators of the Magento on which it will be installed. Be sure to use a namespace which identifies you, and use this namespace for all your extensions.

3. Open a terminal and change the directory to the Magento project root folder.

4. Enable the module by running the two following commands:

   ```
   php bin/magento module:enable
   php bin/magento setup:upgrade
   ```

5. Create the `[extension_path]/registration.php` file and add the following code:

```php
<?php
/**
 * Copyright © 2015 Magento. All rights reserved.
 * See COPYING.txt for license details.
 */

\Magento\Framework\Component\ComponentRegistrar::register(
    \Magento\Framework\Component\ComponentRegistrar::MODULE,
    'Blackbird_TicketBlaster',
    __DIR__
);
```

6. You should see mentions of your new module, as in the following screenshot:

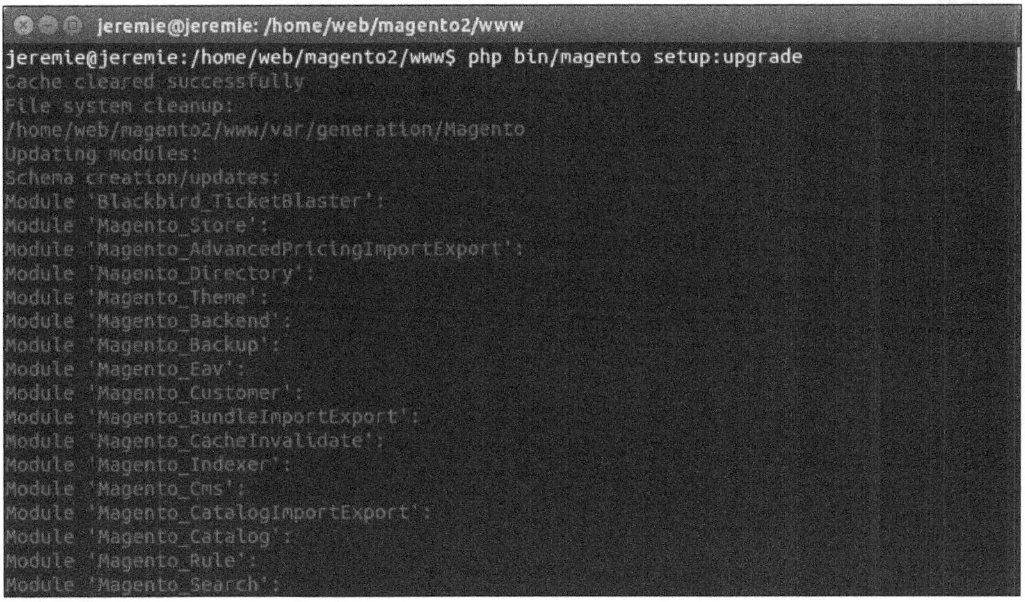

7. You can already check that your module is taken into account by Magento by connecting to the admin and navigating to **Stores | Configuration | Advanced | Advanced | Disable Modules Output**:

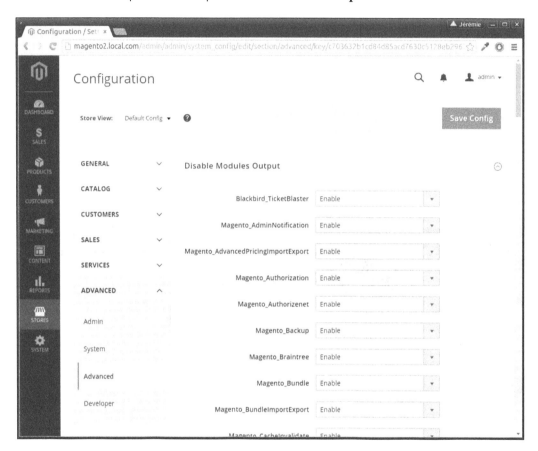

 Be careful: this **Configuration** menu just allows disabling the output of a module and does not deactivate it.

Creating a helper

A helper will (this is not a surprise) *help* you and the extension during development by providing functions that execute little parts of code, such as getting a configuration value, executing generic functions for the extension, or testing the time zone.

Create a `Helper` class of the extension by adding the following code into the `Helper` `[extension_path]/Helper/Event.php`:

 From this point, we shall use `[extension_path]` to represent the path of our extension, which is `app/code/Blackbird/TicketBlaster`.

```php
<?php

namespace Blackbird\TicketBlaster\Helper;

classEvent extends \Magento\Framework\App\Helper\AbstractHelper
{

    /**
     * Create just a useful method for our extension
     *
     * @return bool
     */
public function justAUsefulMethod(){
        // Real code here
        // ...
return true;
    }
}
```

Creating a controller

Now, we will create a `controller` class to handle several issues. In our case, we prepare this `controller` in order to list all events at a venue. Moreover, controllers can get a request from the browser with parameters and dispatch it to the models of our extension.

1. Before coding our `controller`, we need to create a new XML configuration file, in order to declare the new route. Create the `[extension_path]/etc/frontend/routes.xml` file and add the following code:

```xml
<?xml version="1.0"?>
<config xmlns:xsi="http://www.w3.org/2001/XMLSchema-instance" xsi:noNamespaceSchemaLocation="urn:magento:framework:App/etc/routes.xsd">
<router id="standard">
<route id="events" frontName="events">
```

```
<module name="Blackbird_TicketBlaster" />
</route>
</router>
</config>
```

2. Next, create the `[extension_path]/Controller/Index/Index.php` file and add the following code:

```php
<?php

namespace Blackbird\TicketBlaster\Controller\Index;

class Index extends \Magento\Framework\App\Action\Action
{
    /** @var  \Magento\Framework\View\Result\Page */
protected $resultPageFactory;
    /**
     * @param \Magento\Framework\App\Action\Context $context
     */
public function __construct(\Magento\Framework\App\Action\Context
$context,
                            \Magento\Framework\View\Result\
PageFactory $resultPageFactory)
    {
        $this->resultPageFactory = $resultPageFactory;
        parent::__construct($context);
    }

    /**
     * Event Index, shows a list of recent events.
     *
     * @return \Magento\Framework\View\Result\PageFactory
     */
public function execute()
    {
return $this->resultPageFactory->create();
    }
}
```

3. Upgrade your Magento instance by running the following command:

```
php bin/magento setup:upgrade
```

Every time you change anything about the configuration of your extension, you will have to run this command to force Magento to handle your updates.

4. Verify that the URL is accessible by requesting `http://MAGENTO_URL/events/index/index/`:

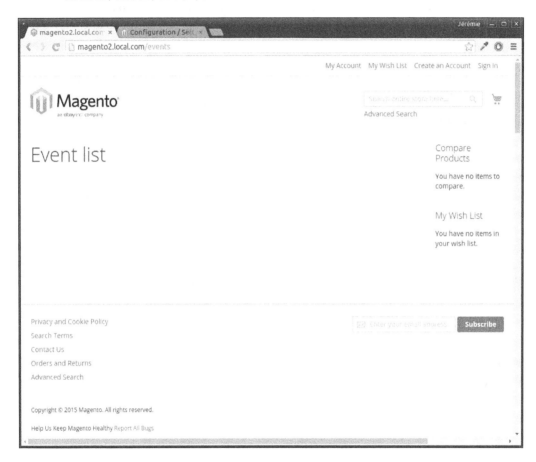

 Controllers are called by Magento when a URL is requested regarding the parameters: `events` corresponds to the `frontName` value in `routes.xml`, `index` is the name of the directory placed in the `Controller` folder, and `index` is the name of the PHP file in the `Index` directory. We will discover later in this chapter how controllers process requests.

Digging into these simple files

You can create this first structure at the beginning of your project, but of course, your project needs will lead you to create some other functionalities we will cover later. For now, it's just a starter. Some extensions require only controllers, others only blocks and models. Just keep in mind this simple explanation:

- Controllers handle frontend and backend requests. They can communicate their data to models if it's needed, and eventually display data to customers or administrators.

- Models handle data, from controllers or from a database. They are the core of your extension, do the main job, and their cap abilities are greater.

- Blocks are here to take charge of the views: every template (`.phtml` file) is handled by a block that contains every necessary method for displaying data.

- Helpers get useful core functions and can be overloaded to add some useful methods.

- XML files, which are in the `etc` folder, declare the module itself and every *core business configuration* of our extension, and can eventually define some default values for the configuration.

- Files that are in the `Setup` folder are files that create or update database tables during the installation of the extension.

Every extension comes in a single and standalone package, which will always be located in `app/code/<EditorName>`. In any case, you can't place your code in `app/code/Magento` (the core folder), because it will be overwritten when Magento is upgraded.

While writing the names of controllers and actions, make sure that they are clear and recognizable, especially by you. Their name must describe what the code does.

You can now test by yourself!

Do not hesitate to read Magento's core code, which informs you about the structure of the modules and how files work together. Make tests by using `var_dump()` to display text and variable values.

During all your Magento development work, use debug logs and the developer mode. These two functionalities will help you a lot and save you a lot of time! Read the `http://magento.com/blog/technical/logging-approach-magento-2` page for explanations about logging; we will use it often in the up coming chapters.

Managing our work with Git source control

Once the project has begun, it may be a good thing to take care of code revision and eventually collaboration with other developers.

Git is a distributed revision control system developed by Linus Torvalds in 2005, initially for Linux kernel development. It has begun to replace the **Subversion** (**SVN**) system in a lot of companies, thanks to its full-fledged repository and independence from network access and a distant server.

As soon as you start to work with other people and developers, the repository must be always available on the Internet. You have two choices to do this: the first is to create a Git repository on your own server (a private server in your organization, or a rented dedicated server), and the second is to use a service that provides a repository for you. In this recipe, we will register our code on Bitbucket.

 GitHub and Sourceforge provide the same services, but Bitbucket offers more free services and is fully integrated with other Atlassian services such as Hipchat or Jira. It is up to you to make your choice according to your needs and environments.

Bitbucket registration

Perform the following steps for Bitbucket registration:

1. Sign up to Bitbucket (`https://bitbucket.org`) by following the instructions on the website:

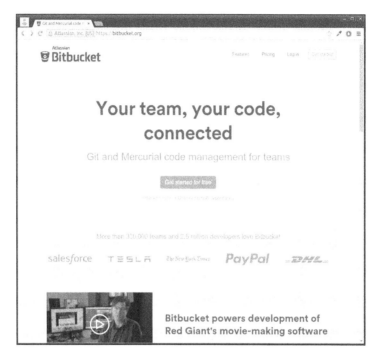

2. In the upper-right corner of any page, click on **Create**, and then click **Create repository**:

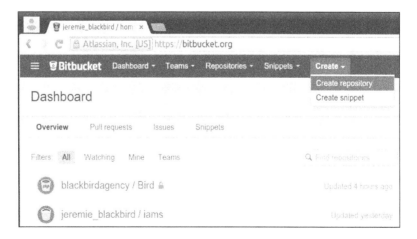

3. Enter your repository name and choose whether your repository will be public or private.

 Check **This is a private repository** if you want to hide your repository from the general public, so that only selected people can see it.

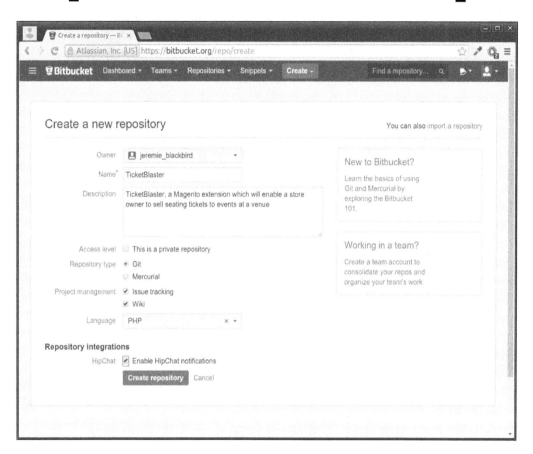

4. That's it for Bitbucket. Keep this window open for future instructions.

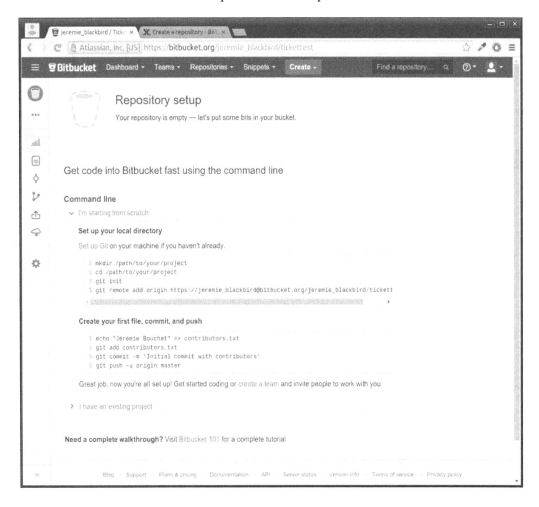

5. Go to your terminal and install Git on your computer by running the following command line:

```
sudo apt-get install git
```

Committing our work

In the following step, we will commit our code to a new repository, and then we will push the repository to Bitbucket:

1. Initialize an empty repository by going to your Magento source folder and running the following command:

   ```
   git init
   ```

2. Check that your repository has been created and is empty:

   ```
   git status
   ```

3. Create a `.gitignore` file in the root of the repository and add the following content to it:

   ```
   #Git ignore for extensions writing
   /app/code/Magento/*
   /dev/tests/
   /lib/
   [...]
   ```

    The source code can be found in the `by-chapter` branch of the Git repository, in the `Chapter1` folder.

4. Verify that the `.gitignore` file is taken into account by running `git status` again:

   ```
   git status
   ```

```
jeremie@jeremie: /home/web/magento2/www/app/code/Blackbird
jeremie@jeremie:/home/web/magento2/www/app/code/Blackbird$ git status
Sur la branche master
Votre branche est à jour avec 'origin/master'.
Modifications qui ne seront pas validées :
  (utilisez "git add/rm <fichier>..." pour mettre à jour ce qui sera validé)
  (utilisez "git checkout -- <fichier>..." pour annuler les modifications dans la copie
de travail)

        modifié :        ../../../.gitignore
        supprimé :       ../../../composer.json
        supprimé :       ../../../composer.lock

Fichiers non suivis:
  (utilisez "git add <fichier>..." pour inclure dans ce qui sera validé)

        ../../../.modman
        ./

aucune modification n'a été ajoutée à la validation (utilisez "git add" ou "git commit -
a")
jeremie@jeremie:/home/web/magento2/www/app/code/Blackbird$
```

5. You can see that only .gitignore is taken into account by Git.

 What happened? In fact, in a Magento project, especially with Magento CE, the source files are always available online and are the same for all. That's why you can presume that each of your collaborators first, and every client next, will run Magento. This is your code, it is unique and important, and that's why your code is the only thing to keep in your repository. Note for later: if you need to add another folder in your repository, just remove the corresponding ignore line.

6. Run the following commands to add and commit the .gitignore file:

```
git add .gitignore
git commit .gitignore -m "Ignoring all resources files"
```

7. Now your repository needs to be filled with the files of our project. Repeat the operation for all the files the extension needs with the command git add <folder | filename>:

```
git -f add app/code/Blackbird/
```

 Note the -f option, to force Git to add the file even if it is stored in an ignored folder. If you don't use this option, Git will inform you that it can't add the file.

8. Commit your additions:

```
git commit -m "Adding the first extension files"
```

9. Link your repository to the Bitbucket repository:

```
git remote add originhttps://YOUR_USERNAME@bitbucket.org/
blackbirdagency/ticket-blaster.git
```

 This line is to modify your repository configuration.

10. Finally, send the files and commit comments to Bitbucket by pushing the repository:

```
git push -u origin master
```

You will find your files by clicking on your repository name on https://bitbucket.org/, proving that the files have been sent and are available for other users.

Take note not to send useless files.

When you are creating an extension, the people who install your code will already have a Magento instance. It is very important to share only the extension files and not Magento and customizable files, which are already modified or installed by your client.

That's why we have chosen to ignore almost all files by default, and to force a git add with the -f option when the file we need to share is placed in an ignored folder.

Discovering other Git servers!

There are others Git storage services online, such as `https://github.com/` or `https://sourceforge.net/`, which offer different storage spaces and different public/private repo policies.

You can create your own private Git server too, which can be dedicated to your company or organization.

Registering dependencies

If your module wants to override some preference values, or just change the default work of a module, you must be able to specify that your configuration must be loaded after the one you override.

In another way, your module could use some class methods defined by other modules and extensions to do its work.

We will discover dependency registering, and we are going to use it for our extension.

Discovering Composer

Composer is a package manager for PHP that provides a standard format for managing dependencies and handling complete complex installation processes. Magento 2 decided to base all platform development on Composer because it's very powerful, open source, and can manage autoloading for third party libraries and code (such as our extension).

We will now see how to use it to manage our extension and its dependencies, which are now published in a public repository on Bitbucket:

1. Create the [extension_path]/composer.json file and add the following code:

```json
{
    "name": "blackbird/ticketblaster",
    "description": "Ticket manager for events",
    "type": "magento2-module",
    "version": "1.0.0",
    "license": [
        "OSL-3.0",
        "AFL-3.0"
    ],
    "require": {
        "magento/magento-composer-installer": "*",
        "magento/catalog":"*"
    },
    "extra": {
        "map": [
            [
                "*",
                "Blackbird/TicketBlaster"
            ]
        ]
    },
    "authors": [
        {
            "name": "Blackbird",
            "homepage": "http://black.bird.eu/",
            "role": "Developer"
        }
    ]
}
```

 The dependencies for our extension are listed in the require key.

2. Commit and push this file to your repository.

3. Update the main Magento 2 `composer.json` file by running the following command:

   `composer config repositories.blackbird vcs https://bitbucket.org/ blackbirdagency/ticket-blaster`

4. Install the extension by running the following command:

   `composer require blackbird/ticketblaster`

 This method is only recommended when you develop private projects, which are not destined to be published. Use Packagist.org registering in other cases!

Discovering packagist

`https://packagist.org/` is the main and default Composer repository. It aggregates public PHP packages installable with Composer.

When you use the Composer binary to add a new extension, the first thing that Composer will do is read the main `composer.json` file of Magento. If your required extension isn't listed or documented, it will ask `https://packagist.org/` to get more information.

In the case of `TicketBlaster`, the extension is published in a public Git repository and we want to share it with everyone who needs it, even if they are not familiar with Composer. The simple way for all your clients to install the extension is by running just one command:

1. Create an account on `https://packagist.org`.

2. Once logged in, submit your package:

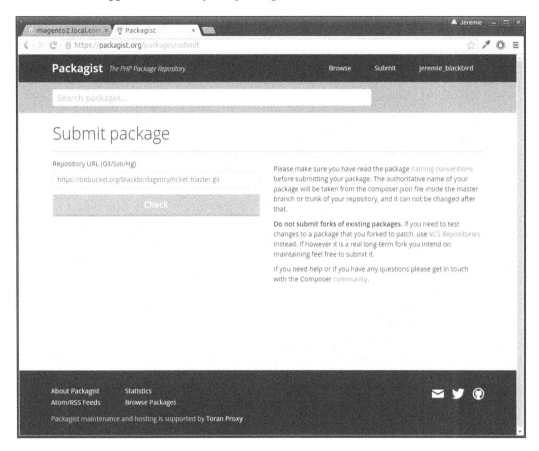

 At this point, Magento 2 hasn't built its package sharing system; it will be launched in a few months.

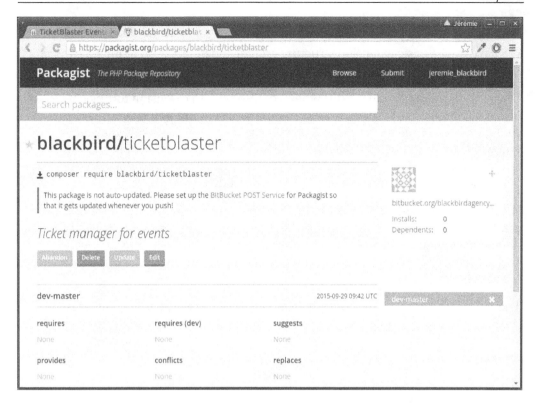

3. Now you just have to run the following command to install your extension:

```
composer require blackbird/ticketblaster
```

> Magento 2 uses Composer to package components and
> product editions. This book cannot look at all the powerful
> functionalities of Composer, so I recommend you read the
> detailed explanation on `http://devdocs.magento.com/`
> `guides/v2.0/extension-dev-guide/composer-`
> `integration.html`, which explains how Magento and
> Composer work together.

Designing TicketBlaster – the backend

We have now a basic extension structure and its dependencies. We must now think about TicketBlaster's structure and functionalities.

One of the most important things when you propose an extension for the community is that it contains the capacity to be configurable; the more you let your clients configure the extension, the more they will use it and the less likely they are to ask you whether something is available or customizable. Think of people who don't know about code development, and think of all the Magento developers who install your extension and don't have enough time to modify it.

We first need to create and manage the events. These events should be able to be created by the administrator and listed in the frontend. Furthermore, the events will have some characteristics, such as a name, a venue, and a date. You can obviously add any field you want for your event, and make it even better by creating a specific list of venues. The event will contain every ticket available for it.

The tickets (the product the customer can buy) will be based on Magento virtual products. But we are going to slightly modify the way we will use these by creating a new product type. This new product type will allow us to link the product to an event.

Creating the table for the events

Perform the following steps to create the table:

1. Create the `[extension_path]/Setup/` folder and then create the `InstallSchema.php` file. Add the following code:

```php
<?php

namespace Blackbird\TicketBlaster\Setup;

use Magento\Framework\Setup\InstallSchemaInterface;
use Magento\Framework\Setup\ModuleContextInterface;
use Magento\Framework\Setup\SchemaSetupInterface;
use Magento\Framework\DB\Ddl\Table;

class InstallSchema implements InstallSchemaInterface
{
[...]
```

The source code can be found in the by-chapter branch
of the Git repository, in the Chapter1 folder.

2. Update the Magento database by running the following command:

```
php bin/magento setup:upgrade
```

 If you want to manually relaunch the SQL installation,
you have to delete the table added by the module and the
line corresponding to TicketBlaster in the setup_module
table, then execute the preceding command again.

3. The extension and its table are installed! To verify this, open your database
interface, for instance phpMyAdmin, and go to the setup_module table:

 This table is really important; Magento uses it to check
whether an extension is installed, and which version.

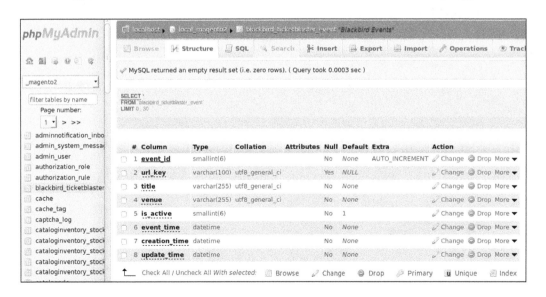

Creating the backend view to list the events

Once the database table has been created, we need to allow the administrator to add, update, and remove events by using the backend.

The first thing we need is a menu to access to the listing of events, so let's create the menu:

1. Create the `[extension_path]/etc/adminhtml/menu.xml` file and add the following code:

```xml
<?xml version="1.0"?>
<config xmlns:xsi="http://www.w3.org/2001/XMLSchema-instance" xsi:
noNamespaceSchemaLocation="urn:magento:module:Magento_Backend:etc/
menu.xsd">
<menu>
<add id="Blackbird_TicketBlaster::ticketblaster"
title="TicketBlaster" module="Blackbird_TicketBlaster"
sortOrder="50" parent="Magento_Backend::content"
resource="Blackbird_TicketBlaster::ticketblaster" />
<add id="Blackbird_TicketBlaster::ticketblaster_
event" title="Events" module="Blackbird_TicketBlaster"
sortOrder="0" parent="Blackbird_TicketBlaster::ticketblaster"
action="ticketblaster/event" resource="Blackbird_
TicketBlaster::ticketblaster_event"/>
</menu>
</config>
```

This simple code will add the menu in the global menu of Magento, in the **Content** main entry:

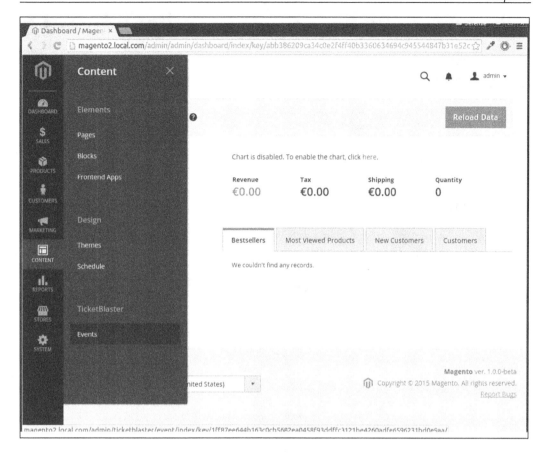

If you click on the **menu** item, you will be redirected to the dashboard, which is completely normal; we haven't created a controller to handle the request. That's what we are going to do now.

2. Create the `[extension_path]/etc/adminhtml/routes.xml` file and add the following code:

```
<?xml version="1.0"?>
<config xmlns:xsi="http://www.w3.org/2001/XMLSchema-instance" xsi
:noNamespaceSchemaLocation="urn:magento:framework:App/etc/routes.
xsd">
<router id="admin">
<route id="ticketblaster" frontName="ticketblaster">
<module name="Blackbird_TicketBlaster" before="Magento_Backend" />
</route>
</router>
</config>
```

3. Create a new folder, `[extension_path]/Controller/Adminhtml/Event`, in which you create the `Index.php` file. Then add the following code:

```php
<?php
namespace Blackbird\TicketBlaster\Controller\Adminhtml\Event;

use Magento\Backend\App\Action\Context;
use Magento\Framework\View\Result\PageFactory;

class Index extends \Magento\Backend\App\Action
{
const ADMIN_RESOURCE = 'Blackbird_TicketBlaster::ticketblaster_
event';

    /**
     * @var PageFactory
     */
protected $resultPageFactory;

    /**
     * @param Context $context
     * @param PageFactory $resultPageFactory
     */
public function __construct(
        Context $context,
        PageFactory $resultPageFactory
    ) {
        parent::__construct($context);
        $this->resultPageFactory = $resultPageFactory;
    }

    /**
     * Index action
     *
     * @return \Magento\Backend\Model\View\Result\Page
     */
public function execute()
    {
        /** @var \Magento\Backend\Model\View\Result\Page
$resultPage */
        $resultPage = $this->resultPageFactory->create();
        $resultPage->setActiveMenu('Blackbird_
TicketBlaster::ticketblaster_event');
        $resultPage->addBreadcrumb(__('Events'), __('Events'));
```

```
        $resultPage->addBreadcrumb(__('Manage Events'), __('Manage
Events'));
        $resultPage->getConfig()->getTitle()->prepend(__
('TicketBlaster Events'));

return $resultPage;
    }
}
```

 Be careful: Magento and folder names are case-sensitive.

The default `execute()` method generates the page. You will get a blank page if you click on the menu item; this is normal, and it is important to ensure you that you get this blank page before continuing. As long as you are redirected or something else, it means that your controller hasn't been read.

 From Step 4 and up to Step 20, there will be nothing to see in the backend. At most, you will have some errors and exceptions. So follow the steps strictly and test by reloading only at the end of the series.

4. Create the `[extension_path]/view/adminhtml/layout` folder.

5. Create the `[extension_path]/view/adminhtml/layout/ticketblaster_event_index.xml` file and add the following code:

```
<page xmlns:xsi="http://www.w3.org/2001/XMLSchema-instance" xsi:n
oNamespaceSchemaLocation="urn:magento:framework:View/Layout/etc/
page_configuration.xsd">
<update handle="styles"/>
<body>
<referenceContainer name="content">
<uiComponent name="ticketblaster_event_listing"/>
</referenceContainer>
</body>
</page>
```

 This code will declare the grid components to load. The filename has to correspond to `<frontname>_<folder_in_controller>_<actionName>`.

6. Create the `[extension_path]/view/adminhtml/ui_component/` folder.

7. Create the `[extension_path]/view/adminhtml/ui_component/`
    `ticketblaster_event_listing.xml` file and add the following code:

    ```xml
    <?xml version="1.0" encoding="UTF-8"?>
    <listing xmlns:xsi="http://www.w3.org/2001/XMLSchema-instance" xs
    i:noNamespaceSchemaLocation="urn:magento:module:Magento_Ui:etc/
    ui_configuration.xsd">
    [...]
    ```

     The source code can be found in the `by-chapter`
    branch of the Git repository, in the `Chapter1` folder.

    This code generates a grid with all these functionalities:

    - **dataSource**: Entity source collection, which allows the loading of all
      the items
    - **filterSearch/filters**: Adds all the filters to the grid
    - **massaction**: Mass action declarations to manipulate items
    - **paging**: Pagination configuration
    - **columns**: Lists all the columns we want to display and their
      configurations, such as type, draggable, align, label, and so on

8. Create the `[extension_path]/Controller/Adminhtml/Event/`
    `AbstractMassStatus.php` file and add the following code:

    ```php
    <?php

    namespace Blackbird\TicketBlaster\Controller\Adminhtml\Event;

    use Magento\Framework\Model\Resource\Db\Collection\
    AbstractCollection;
    use Magento\Framework\Controller\ResultFactory;

    /**
     * Class AbstractMassStatus
     */
    class AbstractMassStatus extends \Magento\Backend\App\Action
    {
    [...]
    ```

The source code can be found in the by-chapter branch of the Git repository, in the Chapter1 folder.

This code allows us to handle our mass actions in the status field.

9. Create the [extension_path]/Controller/Adminhtml/Event/ MassDisable.php file and add the following code:

```php
<?php

namespace Blackbird\TicketBlaster\Controller\Adminhtml\Event;

use Blackbird\TicketBlaster\Controller\Adminhtml\Event\
AbstractMassStatus;

/**
 * Class MassDisable
 */
class MassDisable extends AbstractMassStatus
{
    /**
     * Field id
     */
    const ID_FIELD = 'event_id';

    /**
     * Resource collection
     *
     * @var string
     */
    protected $collection = 'Blackbird\TicketBlaster\Model\Resource\
Event\Collection';

    /**
     * Event model
     *
     * @var string
     */
    protected $model = 'Blackbird\TicketBlaster\Model\Event';

    /**
     * Event disable status
     *
```

```
     * @var boolean
     */
protected $status = false;
}
```

10. Create the [extension_path]/Controller/Adminhtml/Event/
    MassEnable.php file and add the following code:

```php
<?php

namespace Blackbird\TicketBlaster\Controller\Adminhtml\Event;

use Blackbird\TicketBlaster\Controller\Adminhtml\Event\
AbstractMassStatus;

/**
 * Class MassEnable
 */
class MassEnable extends AbstractMassStatus
{
    /**
     * Field id
     */
    const ID_FIELD = 'event_id';

    /**
     * Resource collection
     *
     * @var string
     */
    protected $collection = 'Blackbird\TicketBlaster\Model\Resource\
Event\Collection';

    /**
     * Event model
     *
     * @var string
     */
    protected $model = 'Blackbird\TicketBlaster\Model\Event';

    /**
     * Event enable status
     *
     * @var boolean
```

```
        */
    protected $status = true;
    }
```

11. Create the [extension_path]/Controller/Adminhtml/Event/
    MassDelete.php file and add the following code:

```php
<?php

namespace Blackbird\TicketBlaster\Controller\Adminhtml\Event;
```

```
    [...]
```

> The source code can be found in the by-chapter
> branch of the Git repository, in the Chapter1 folder.
> This file handles our mass action to delete several items
> at the same time.

12. Create the [extension_path]/Controller/Adminhtml/Event/Delete.php
    file and add the following code:

```php
<?php

namespace Blackbird\TicketBlaster\Controller\Adminhtml\Event;

use Magento\Backend\App\Action;
use Magento\TestFramework\ErrorLog\Logger;

class Delete extends \Magento\Backend\App\Action
{

    /**
     * @param Action\Context $context
     */
    public function __construct(Action\Context $context)
    {
        parent::__construct($context);
    }

    /**
     * {@inheritdoc}
     */
```

```php
protected function _isAllowed()
    {
return $this->_authorization->isAllowed('Blackbird_
TicketBlaster::ticketblaster_event_delete');
    }

    /**
     * Delete action
     *
     * @return \Magento\Framework\Controller\ResultInterface
     */
public function execute()
    {
        /** @var \Magento\Backend\Model\View\Result\Redirect
$resultRedirect */
        $resultRedirect = $this->resultRedirectFactory->create();
        // check if we know what should be deleted
        $id = $this->getRequest()->getParam('event_id');
if ($id) {
try {
                // init model and delete
                $model = $this->_objectManager->create('Blackbird\
TicketBlaster\Model\Event');
                $model->load($id);
                $model->delete();
                // display success message
                $this->messageManager->addSuccess(__('You deleted
the event.'));
                // go to grid
return $resultRedirect->setPath('*/*/');
            } catch (\Exception $e) {
                // display error message
                $this->messageManager->addError($e->getMessage());
                // go back to edit form
return $resultRedirect->setPath('*/*/edit', ['event_id' => $id]);
            }
        }
        // display error message
        $this->messageManager->addError(__('We can\'t find a event
to delete.'));
        // go to grid
return $resultRedirect->setPath('*/*/');
    }
}
```

This code handles the deletion of one piece of content at a time. It will also be used in the edit page.

13. Create the `[extension_path]/Model/Event.php` file and add the following code:

```php
<?php

namespace Blackbird\TicketBlaster\Model;

use Blackbird\TicketBlaster\Api\Data\EventInterface;
use Magento\Framework\Object\IdentityInterface;

class Event extends \Magento\Framework\Model\AbstractModel
implements EventInterface, IdentityInterface
{

[...]
```

 The source code can be found in the by-chapter branch of the Git repository, in the Chapter1 folder. This code declares our model for handling our events.

14. Create the `[extension_path]/Model/Resource/Event.php` file and add the following code:

```php
<?php

namespace Blackbird\TicketBlaster\Model\Resource;

class Event extends \Magento\Framework\Model\Resource\Db\
AbstractDb
{
    [...]
```

 The source code can be found in the by-chapter branch of the Git repository, in the Chapter1 folder. This class declares our link between the model and the database.

15. Create the [extension_path]/Model/Resource/Event/Collection.php file and add the following code:

```php
<?php

namespace Blackbird\TicketBlaster\Model\Resource\Event;

class Collection extends \Magento\Framework\Model\Resource\Db\
Collection\AbstractCollection
{
    /**
     * Define resource model
     *
     * @return void
     */
    protected function _construct()
    {
        $this->_init('Blackbird\TicketBlaster\Model\Event',
'Blackbird\TicketBlaster\Model\Resource\Event');
    }

}
```

 This code declares our collection of content of the Event type.

16. Create the [extension_path]/Model/Event/Source/IsActive.php file and add the following code:

```php
<?php

namespace Blackbird\TicketBlaster\Model\Event\Source;

class IsActive implements \Magento\Framework\Data\
OptionSourceInterface {

    /**
     * @var \Blackbird\TicketBlaster\Model\Event
     */
    protected $_event;

    /**
     * Constructor
     *
```

```
       * @param \Blackbird\TicketBlaster\Model\Event $event
       */
     public function __construct(\Blackbird\TicketBlaster\Model\Event
     $event) {
           $this->_event = $event;
       }


       /**
        * Get options
        *
        * @return array
        */
     public function toOptionArray() {
           $options[] = ['label' => '', 'value' => ''];
           $availableOptions = $this->_event->getAvailableStatuses();
     foreach ($availableOptions as $key => $value) {
               $options[] = [
                   'label' => $value,
                   'value' => $key,
               ];
           }
     return $options;
       }


     }
```

 This code lists the available statuses to be used in
the grid.

17. Create the `[extension_path]/Api/Data/EventInterface.php` file and add
    the following code:

```php
<?php

namespace Blackbird\TicketBlaster\Api\Data;

interface EventInterface
{
const EVENT_ID        = 'event_id';
const URL_KEY         = 'url_key';
const TITLE           = 'title';
const VENUE           = 'venue';
const EVENT_TIME       = 'event_time';
```

```
const CREATION_TIME = 'creation_time';
const UPDATE_TIME   = 'update_time';
const IS_ACTIVE     = 'is_active';

[...]
```

The source code can be found in the by-chapter branch of the GIT repository, in the Chapter1 folder.

This code lists all the methods available for an API to use in Magento. This part will be studied later in this book.

18. Create the [extension_path]/etc/acl.xml file and add the following code:

```xml
<?xml version="1.0"?>
<config xmlns:xsi="http://www.w3.org/2001/XMLSchema-instance"
xsi:noNamespaceSchemaLocation=" urn:magento:framework:Acl/etc/acl.
xsd">
<acl>
<resources>
<resource id="Magento_Backend::admin">
<resource id="Magento_Backend::content">
<resource id="Blackbird_TicketBlaster::ticketblaster"
title="TicketBlaster" sortOrder="10" >
<resource id="Blackbird_TicketBlaster::ticketblaster_event"
title="Events" sortOrder="40">
<resource id="Blackbird_TicketBlaster::ticketblaster_event_save"
title="Save" sortOrder="10" />
<resource id="Blackbird_TicketBlaster::ticketblaster_event_delete"
title="Delete" sortOrder="20" />
</resource>
</resource>
</resource>
</resource>
</resources>
</acl>
</config>
```

This code lists all the permissions that can be used to restrict access for specific users in the admin panel.

19. Create the [extension_path]/etc/di.xml file and add the following code:

```xml
<?xml version="1.0"?>
<config xmlns:xsi="http://www.w3.org/2001/XMLSchema-instance"
xsi:noNamespaceSchemaLocation=" urn:magento:framework:ObjectManag
er/etc/config.xsd">
<preference for="Blackbird\TicketBlaster\Api\Data\EventInterface"
type="Blackbird\TicketBlaster\Model\Event" />
<virtualType name="EventGridFilterPool" type="Magento\Framework\
View\Element\UiComponent\DataProvider\FilterPool">
<arguments>
<argument name="appliers" xsi:type="array">
<item name="regular" xsi:type="object">Magento\Framework\View\
Element\UiComponent\DataProvider\RegularFilter</item>
<item name="fulltext" xsi:type="object">Magento\Framework\View\
Element\UiComponent\DataProvider\FulltextFilter</item>
</argument>
</arguments>
</virtualType>
<virtualType name="EventGridDataProvider" type="Magento\Framework\
View\Element\UiComponent\DataProvider\DataProvider">
<arguments>
<argument name="collection" xsi:type="object"
shared="false">Blackbird\TicketBlaster\Model\Resource\Event\
Collection</argument>
<argument name="filterPool" xsi:type="object" shared="false">Event
GridFilterPool</argument>
</arguments>
</virtualType>
</config>
```

 This XML code declares some virtual types that provide filtered data to the grid.

20. Create the [extension_path]/Ui/Component/Listing/Column/
EventActions.php file and add the following code:

```php
<?php

namespace Blackbird\TicketBlaster\Ui\Component\Listing\Column;

use Magento\Framework\View\Element\UiComponent\ContextInterface;
use Magento\Framework\View\Element\UiComponentFactory;
use Magento\Ui\Component\Listing\Columns\Column;
```

```php
use Magento\Framework\UrlInterface;

class EventActions extends Column
{
    /** Url path */
    const TICKETBLASTER_URL_PATH_EDIT = 'ticketblaster/event/edit';
    const TICKETBLASTER_URL_PATH_DELETE = 'ticketblaster/event/
delete';

    /** @var UrlInterface */
    protected $urlBuilder;

    /**
     * @var string
     */
    private $editUrl;

    /**
     * @param ContextInterface $context
     * @param UiComponentFactory $uiComponentFactory
     * @param UrlInterface $urlBuilder
     * @param array $components
     * @param array $data
     * @param string $editUrl
     */
    public function __construct(
        ContextInterface $context,
        UiComponentFactory $uiComponentFactory,
        UrlInterface $urlBuilder,
array $components = [],
array $data = [],
        $editUrl = self::TICKETBLASTER_URL_PATH_EDIT
    ) {
        $this->urlBuilder = $urlBuilder;
        $this->editUrl = $editUrl;
        parent::__construct($context, $uiComponentFactory,
$components, $data);
    }

    /**
     * Prepare Data Source
     *
     * @param array $dataSource
```

```
        * @return void
        */
public function prepareDataSource(array & $dataSource)
    {
if (isset($dataSource['data']['items'])) {
foreach ($dataSource['data']['items'] as & $item) {
                $name = $this->getData('name');
if (isset($item['event_id'])) {
                    $item[$name]['edit'] = [
                        'href' => $this->urlBuilder->getUrl($this-
>editUrl, ['event_id' => $item['event_id']]),
                        'label' => __('Edit')
                    ];
                    $item[$name]['delete'] = [
                        'href' => $this->urlBuilder-
>getUrl(self::TICKETBLASTER_URL_PATH_DELETE, ['event_id' =>
$item['event_id']]),
                        'label' => __('Delete'),
                        'confirm' => [
                            'title' => __('Delete "${ $.$data.
title }"'),
                            'message' => __('Are you sure you
wan\'t to delete a "${ $.$data.title }" record?')
                        ]
                    ];
                }
            }
        }
    }
}
```

 This class handles the action column of our grid by adding two links: delete and edit.

21. Update Magento by running the following command:

```
php bin/magento setup:upgrade
```

 This command, which we use a lot, is very important during Magento development: it clears the cache, upgrades the DB data and schema, generates interceptors and factories, and more!

Hurrah! We can reload our page to see the grid:

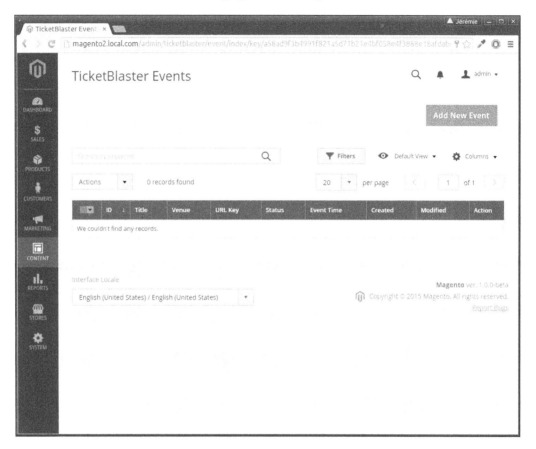

Summary

We now have all the necessary bases for writing an efficient extension that can already do a lot of work, such as saving data and managing it. It only lacks the ability for users to manage this data, and that's exactly what we will provide in the following chapter.

All the code in this book is freely available here:
`https://bitbucket.org/blackbirdagency/ticket-blaster`.
Do not hesitate to download it, update it, and maybe even send new modifications!

2
Deeper Extension Development

The previous chapter taught us the basics of extension development. In this chapter, we will see how powerful your code can be, by providing for future users some useful forms in the admin area and a user-friendly interface in the frontend. This is the only good way to make your extension different: offering the best experience to your customers and their customers.

Briefly, we will cover the following:

- Creating the backend forms to manage events
- Designing the `TicketBlaster` module's frontend

Creating the backend forms to manage events

In the previous chapter, we wrote all the code to store event data in our specific module's table. We can now list our events, but we cannot create or edit them. Test yourself by clicking on the **Add New Event** button; you will be redirected to the dashboard. We are therefore going to create our events by performing the following steps:

1. Create the `[extension_path]/Controller/Adminhtml/Event/NewAction.php` file and add this code:

   ```php
   <?php

   namespace Blackbird\TicketBlaster\Controller\Adminhtml\Event;

   class NewAction extends \Magento\Backend\App\Action
   ```

```
{
    /**
     * @var \Magento\Backend\Model\View\Result\Forward
     */
    protected $resultForwardFactory;

    /**
     * @param \Magento\Backend\App\Action\Context $context
     * @param \Magento\Backend\Model\View\Result\ForwardFactory
$resultForwardFactory
     */
    public function __construct(
        \Magento\Backend\App\Action\Context $context,
        \Magento\Backend\Model\View\Result\ForwardFactory
$resultForwardFactory
    ) {
        $this->resultForwardFactory = $resultForwardFactory;
        parent::__construct($context);
    }

    /**
     * {@inheritdoc}
     */
    protected function _isAllowed()
    {
return $this->_authorization->isAllowed('Blackbird_
TicketBlaster::ticketblaster_event_save');
    }

    /**
     * Forward to edit
     *
     * @return \Magento\Backend\Model\View\Result\Forward
     */
    public function execute()
    {
        /** @var \Magento\Backend\Model\View\Result\Forward
$resultForward */
        $resultForward = $this->resultForwardFactory->create();
return $resultForward->forward('edit');
    }
}
```

This class and its `execute()` method forwards the user to the edit action.

2. Create the `[extension_path]/Controller/Adminhtml/Event/Edit.php` file and add the following code:

```php
<?php

namespace Blackbird\TicketBlaster\Controller\Adminhtml\Event;

use Magento\Backend\App\Action;

class Edit extends \Magento\Backend\App\Action
{
    /**
     * Core registry
     *
     * @var \Magento\Framework\Registry
     */
    protected $_coreRegistry = null;

    /**
     * @var \Magento\Framework\View\Result\PageFactory
     */
    protected $resultPageFactory;

    /**
     * @param Action\Context $context
     * @param \Magento\Framework\View\Result\PageFactory
$resultPageFactory
     * @param \Magento\Framework\Registry $registry
     */
    public function __construct(
        Action\Context $context,
        \Magento\Framework\View\Result\PageFactory
$resultPageFactory,
        \Magento\Framework\Registry $registry
    ) {
        $this->resultPageFactory = $resultPageFactory;
        $this->_coreRegistry = $registry;
        parent::__construct($context);
    }

    /**
     * {@inheritdoc}
```

```
        */
protected function _isAllowed()
    {
return $this->_authorization->isAllowed('Blackbird_
TicketBlaster::ticketblaster_event_save');
    }

    /**
     * Init actions
     *
     * @return \Magento\Backend\Model\View\Result\Page
     */
protected function _initAction()
    {
        // load layout, set active menu and breadcrumbs
        /** @var \Magento\Backend\Model\View\Result\Page
$resultPage */
        $resultPage = $this->resultPageFactory->create();
        $resultPage->setActiveMenu('Blackbird_
TicketBlaster::ticketblaster_event')
            ->addBreadcrumb(__('Event'), __('Event'))
            ->addBreadcrumb(__('Manage Events'), __('Manage
Events'));
return $resultPage;
    }

    /**
     * Edit event
     *
     * @return \Magento\Backend\Model\View\Result\Page|\Magento\
Backend\Model\View\Result\Redirect
     * @SuppressWarnings(PHPMD.NPathComplexity)
     */
public function execute()
    {
        $id = $this->getRequest()->getParam('event_id');
        $model = $this->_objectManager->create('Blackbird\
TicketBlaster\Model\Event');

if ($id) {
            $model->load($id);
if (!$model->getId()) {
                $this->messageManager->addError(__('This event no
longer exists.'));
                /** \Magento\Backend\Model\View\Result\Redirect
$resultRedirect */
```

```
                $resultRedirect = $this->resultRedirectFactory-
>create();

return $resultRedirect->setPath('*/*/');
            }
        }

        $data = $this->_objectManager->get('Magento\Backend\Model\
Session')->getFormData(true);
if (!empty($data)) {
            $model->setData($data);
        }

        $this->_coreRegistry->register('ticketblaster_event',
$model);

        /** @var \Magento\Backend\Model\View\Result\Page
$resultPage */
        $resultPage = $this->_initAction();
        $resultPage->addBreadcrumb(
            $id ? __('Edit Event') : __('New Event'),
            $id ? __('Edit Event') : __('New Event')
        );
        $resultPage->getConfig()->getTitle()->prepend(__
('Events'));
        $resultPage->getConfig()->getTitle()
            ->prepend($model->getId() ? $model->getTitle() : __
('New Event'));

return $resultPage;
    }
}
```

 This `Controller` handles the form for the editing and creation of the event.

3. Create the `[extension_path]/Controller/Adminhtml/Event/Save.php` file and add the following code:

```php
<?php

namespace Blackbird\TicketBlaster\Controller\Adminhtml\Event;

use Magento\Backend\App\Action;
```

```
use Magento\TestFramework\ErrorLog\Logger;

class Save extends \Magento\Backend\App\Action
{

    /**
     * @param Action\Context $context
     */
    public function __construct(Action\Context $context)
    {
        parent::__construct($context);
    }

    /**
     * {@inheritdoc}
     */
    protected function _isAllowed()
    {
    return $this->_authorization->isAllowed('Blackbird_
    TicketBlaster::ticketblaster_event_save');
    }

    /**
     * Save action
     *
     * @return \Magento\Framework\Controller\ResultInterface
     */
    public function execute()
    {
        $data = $this->getRequest()->getPostValue();
        /** @var \Magento\Backend\Model\View\Result\Redirect
$resultRedirect */
        $resultRedirect = $this->resultRedirectFactory->create();
if ($data) {
            /** @var \Blackbird\TicketBlaster\Model\Event $model
*/
            $model = $this->_objectManager->create('Blackbird\
TicketBlaster\Model\Event');

            $id = $this->getRequest()->getParam('event_id');
if ($id) {
                $model->load($id);
            }

            $model->setData($data);

            $this->_eventManager->dispatch(
```

```
                   'ticketblaster_event_prepare_save',
                   ['event' => $model, 'request' => $this-
>getRequest()]
               );

    try {

                $model->save();
                $this->messageManager->addSuccess(__('You saved
this Event.'));
                $this->_objectManager->get('Magento\Backend\Model\
Session')->setFormData(false);
    if ($this->getRequest()->getParam('back')) {
    return $resultRedirect->setPath('*/*/edit', ['event_id' => $model-
>getId(), '_current' => true]);
                }
    return $resultRedirect->setPath('*/*/');
            } catch (\Magento\Framework\Exception\
LocalizedException $e) {
                $this->messageManager->addError($e->getMessage());
            } catch (\RuntimeException $e) {
                $this->messageManager->addError($e->getMessage());
            } catch (\Exception $e) {
                $this->messageManager->addException($e, __
('Something went wrong while saving the event.'));
                }

                $this->_getSession()->setFormData($data);
    return $resultRedirect->setPath('*/*/edit', ['event_id' => $this-
>getRequest()->getParam('event_id')]);
            }
    return $resultRedirect->setPath('*/*/');
        }
    }
```

 This class saves our model in the database and redirects the user to the grid.

4. Create the [extension_path]/view/adminhmlt/layout/ticketblaster_
   event_edit.xml file and add the following code:

   ```
   <page xmlns:xsi="http://www.w3.org/2001/XMLSchema-instance" xs
   i:noNamespaceSchemaLocation="../../../../../../../lib/internal/
   Magento/Framework/View/Layout/etc/page_configuration.xsd">
   <update handle="editor"/>
   <body>
   ```

```
<referenceContainer name="content">
<block class="Blackbird\TicketBlaster\Block\Adminhtml\Event\Edit"
name="ticketblaster.event.edit"/>
</referenceContainer>
</body>
</page>
```

 This layout adds the form in the main container of the editing page.

5. Create the `[extension_path]/Block/Adminhtml/Event/Edit/Form.php` file and add the following code:

```php
<?php

namespace Blackbird\TicketBlaster\Block\Adminhtml\Event\Edit;

/**
 * Adminhtml event edit form
 */
class Form extends \Magento\Backend\Block\Widget\Form\Generic
{

    /**
     * @var \Magento\Store\Model\System\Store
     */
    protected $_systemStore;

    /**
     * @param \Magento\Backend\Block\Template\Context $context
     * @param \Magento\Framework\Registry $registry
     * @param \Magento\Framework\Data\FormFactory $formFactory
     * @param \Magento\Cms\Model\Wysiwyg\Config $wysiwygConfig
     * @param \Magento\Store\Model\System\Store $systemStore
     * @param array $data
     */
    public function __construct(
        \Magento\Backend\Block\Template\Context $context,
        \Magento\Framework\Registry $registry,
        \Magento\Framework\Data\FormFactory $formFactory,
        \Magento\Store\Model\System\Store $systemStore,
array $data = []
    ) {
        $this->_systemStore = $systemStore;
```

```php
        parent::__construct($context, $registry, $formFactory,
$data);
    }

    /**
     * Init form
     *
     * @return void
     */
protected function _construct()
    {
        parent::_construct();
        $this->setId('event_form');
        $this->setTitle(__('Event Information'));
    }

    /**
     * Prepare form
     *
     * @return $this
     */
protected function _prepareForm()
    {
        /** @var \Blackbird\TicketBlaster\Model\Event $model */
        $model = $this->_coreRegistry->registry('ticketblaster_
event');

        /** @var \Magento\Framework\Data\Form $form */
        $form = $this->_formFactory->create(
            ['data' => ['id' => 'edit_form', 'action' => $this-
>getData('action'), 'method' => 'post']]
        );

        $form->setHtmlIdPrefix('event_');

        $fieldset = $form->addFieldset(
            'base_fieldset',
['legend' => __('General Information'), 'class' => 'fieldset-
wide']
        );

if ($model->getEventId()) {
            $fieldset->addField('event_id', 'hidden', ['name' =>
'event_id']);
```

```
        }

        $fieldset->addField(
            'title',
            'text',
['name' => 'title', 'label' => __('Title'), 'title' => __
('Title'), 'required' => true]
        );

        $fieldset->addField(
            'venue',
            'text',
['name' => 'venue', 'label' => __('Venue'), 'venue' => __
('Venue'), 'required' => true]
        );

        $dateFormat = $this->_localeDate->getDateFormat(\
IntlDateFormatter::SHORT);
        $timeFormat = $this->_localeDate->getTimeFormat(\
IntlDateFormatter::SHORT);
        $fieldset->addField(
            'event_time',
            'date',
            [
                'label' => __('Event Time'),
                'title' => __('Event Time'),
                'name' => 'event_time',
                'date_format' => $dateFormat,
                'time_format' => $timeFormat,
                'required' => true
            ]
        );

        $fieldset->addField(
            'url_key',
            'text',
            [
                'name' => 'url_key',
                'label' => __('URL Key'),
                'title' => __('URL Key'),
                'required' => true,
                'class' => 'validate-xml-identifier'
            ]
```

```
        );

        $fieldset->addField(
            'is_active',
            'select',
            [
                'label' => __('Status'),
                'title' => __('Status'),
                'name' => 'is_active',
                'required' => true,
                'options' => ['1' => __('Enabled'), '0' => __
('Disabled')]
            ]
        );
if (!$model->getId()) {
            $model->setData('is_active', '1');
        }


        $form->setValues($model->getData());
        $form->setUseContainer(true);
        $this->setForm($form);

return parent::_prepareForm();
    }
}
```

 This class determines which fields can be modified by the user.

6. Create the `[extension_path]/Block/Adminhtml/Event/Edit.php` file and add the following code:

```php
<?php
namespace Blackbird\TicketBlaster\Block\Adminhtml\Event;

class Edit extends \Magento\Backend\Block\Widget\Form\Container
{
    /**
     * Core registry
     *
     * @var \Magento\Framework\Registry
```

```
    */
protected $_coreRegistry = null;

    /**
     * @param \Magento\Backend\Block\Widget\Context $context
     * @param \Magento\Framework\Registry $registry
     * @param array $data
     */
public function __construct(
        \Magento\Backend\Block\Widget\Context $context,
        \Magento\Framework\Registry $registry,
array $data = []
    ) {
        $this->_coreRegistry = $registry;
        parent::__construct($context, $data);
    }

    /**
     * Initialize event edit block
     *
     * @return void
     */
protected function _construct()
    {
        $this->_objectId = 'event_id';
        $this->_blockGroup = 'Blackbird_TicketBlaster';
        $this->_controller = 'adminhtml_event';

        parent::_construct();

if ($this->_isAllowedAction('Blackbird_
TicketBlaster::ticketblaster_event_save')) {
            $this->buttonList->update('save', 'label', __('Save
Event'));
            $this->buttonList->add(
                'saveandcontinue',
                [
                    'label' => __('Save and Continue Edit'),
                    'class' => 'save',
                    'data_attribute' => [
                        'mage-init' => [
```

```
                                   'button' => ['event' =>
'saveAndContinueEdit', 'target' => '#edit_form'],
                    ],
                ]
            ],
            -100
        );
    } else {
        $this->buttonList->remove('save');
    }


if ($this->_isAllowedAction('Blackbird_
TicketBlaster::ticketblaster_event_delete')) {
        $this->buttonList->update('delete', 'label', __
('Delete Event'));
    } else {
        $this->buttonList->remove('delete');
    }
}

/**
 * Retrieve text for header element depending on loaded event
 *
 * @return \Magento\Framework\Phrase
 */
public function getHeaderText()
{
if ($this->_coreRegistry->registry('ticketblaster_event')-
>getId()) {
return __("Edit Event '%1'", $this->escapeHtml($this->_
coreRegistry->registry('ticketblaster_event')->getTitle()));
    } else {
return __('New Event');
    }
}

/**
 * Check permission for passed action
 *
 * @param string $resourceId
 * @return bool
 */
protected function _isAllowedAction($resourceId)
{
```

```
    return $this->_authorization->isAllowed($resourceId);
    }

    /**
     * Getter of url for "Save and Continue" button
     * tab_id will be replaced by desired by JS later
     *
     * @return string
     */
    protected function _getSaveAndContinueUrl()
    {
        return $this->getUrl('ticketblaster/*/save', ['_current'
=> true, 'back' => 'edit', 'active_tab' => '']);
    }
}
```

 This class wraps the form and adds the action buttons for the form.

7. Update **Magento** by running the following command:

```
php bin/magento setup:upgrade
```

Hurrah! We can click on **New Event** on our grid page to see the form:

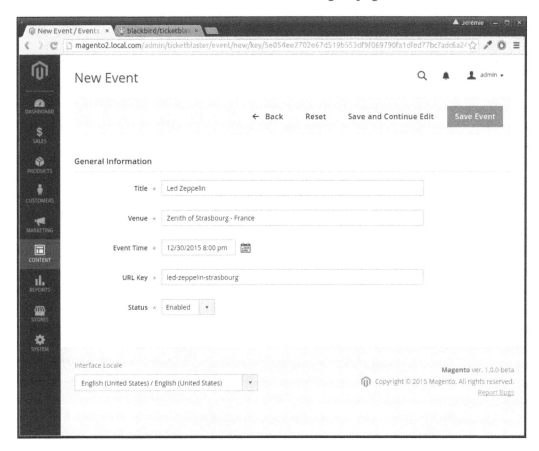

Now, we can create, edit, save, and delete as many events as we want. Create one or two events, so that you have a little database for the next steps.

Finally, your extensions folder should look like this:

```
▼ Blackbird TicketBlaster [ticket-blaster master]
  ▼ app
    ▼ code
      ▼ Blackbird
        ▼ TicketBlaster
          ▼ Model
            ▼ Event
              ▼ Source
                ▶ IsActive.php
            ▼ Resource
              ▼ Event
                ▶ Collection.php
              ▶ Event.php
            ▶ Event.php
          ▼ Setup
            ▶ InstallSchema.php
          ▼ Api
            ▼ Data
              ▶ EventInterface.php
          ▼ Block
            ▼ Adminhtml
              ▼ Event
                ▼ Edit
                  Form.php
                Edit.php
              EventList.php
              EventView.php
          ▼ Controller
            ▼ Adminhtml
              ▼ Event
                AbstractMassStatus.php
                Delete.php
                Edit.php
                Index.php
                MassDelete.php
                MassDisable.php
                MassEnable.php
                NewAction.php
                Save.php
```

Designing the TicketBlaster module's frontend

Ok, now we can create events, except that we cannot show them to our customers!

We will see that the layout can be prepared and packaged in the extension in order to provide the best integration for customers.

Declaring the layouts

The following steps show how to declare layouts:

1. Create the `[extension_path]/view/frontend/layout/events_index_index.xml` file and add the following code:

```
<page xmlns:xsi="http://www.w3.org/2001/XMLSchema-instance" xs
i:noNamespaceSchemaLocation="../../../../../../../lib/internal/
Magento/Framework/View/Layout/etc/page_configuration.xsd">
<body>
<referenceContainer name="content">
<block class="Blackbird\TicketBlaster\Block\EventList"
name="event.list" template="Blackbird_TicketBlaster::list.phtml"
/>
</referenceContainer>
</body>
</page>
```

 This layout file adds the block to list our events in the main container of the page.

2. Create the `[extension_path]/view/frontend/layout/events_view_index.xml` file and add the following code:

```
<page xmlns:xsi="http://www.w3.org/2001/XMLSchema-instance" xs
i:noNamespaceSchemaLocation="../../../../../../../lib/internal/
Magento/Framework/View/Layout/etc/page_configuration.xsd">
<body>
<referenceContainer name="content">
<block class="Blackbird\TicketBlaster\Block\EventView"
name="event.view" template="Blackbird_TicketBlaster::view.phtml"
/>
</referenceContainer>
</body>
</page>
```

 This layout file adds the block to view a details page for one event in the main container of the page.

Creating a template file

Follow these steps to create a template file:

1. Create the `[extension_path]/view/frontend/templates/list.phtml` file and add the following content in the template file:

```php
<?php /** @var $block \Blackbird\TicketBlaster\Block\EventList */
?>
<h1><?php echo __('Event list') ?></h1>

<ul class="ticketblaster-events-list">

<?php /** @var $event \Blackbird\TicketBlaster\Model\Event */ ?>
<?php foreach ($block->getEvents() as $event): ?>
<li class="ticketblaster-event-list-item">
<h3 class="ticketblaster-event-item-title">
<a href="<?php echo $event->getUrl() ?>"><?php echo $event-
>getTitle() ?></a>
</h3>

<div class="ticketblaster-event-item-content">
<?php echo $event->getContent(); ?>
</div>

<div class="ticketblaster-event-item-meta">
<strong><?php echo __('Event time:') ?></strong><?php echo $event-
>getEventTime() ?>
</div>
</li>
<?php endforeach; ?>

</ul>
```

2. Create the `[extension_path]/view/frontend/templates/view.phtml` file and add the following content in the template file:

```php
<?php
    /** @var $block \Blackbird\TicketBlaster\Block\EventView */
    /** @var $event \Blackbird\TicketBlaster\Model\Event */

    $event = $block->getEvent();
?>

<h1 class="ticketblaster-event-item-title"><?php echo $event-
>getTitle() ?></h1>
```

```
<div class="ticketblaster-event-item-content">
<strong><?php echo __('Event time:') ?></strong><?php echo $event-
>getEventTime(); ?><br/>
<?php echo $event->getVenue(); ?><br/>
</div>
```

Creating the block files

The following steps will declare the necessary blocks:

1. Create the `[extension_path]/Block/EventList.php` file and add the following content:

```php
<?php
namespace Blackbird\TicketBlaster\Block;
use Blackbird\TicketBlaster\Api\Data\EventInterface;
use Blackbird\TicketBlaster\Model\Resource\Event\Collection as
EventCollection;

class EventList extends \Magento\Framework\View\Element\Template
implements \Magento\Framework\Object\IdentityInterface
{
    /**
     * Construct
     *
     * @param \Magento\Framework\View\Element\Template\Context
$context
     * @param \Blackbird\TicketBlaster\Model\Resource\Event\
CollectionFactory $eventCollectionFactory,
     * @param array $data
     */
public function __construct(
        \Magento\Framework\View\Element\Template\Context $context,
        \Blackbird\TicketBlaster\Model\Resource\Event\
CollectionFactory $eventCollectionFactory,
array $data = []
    ) {
        parent::__construct($context, $data);
        $this->_eventCollectionFactory = $eventCollectionFactory;
    }

    /**
     * @return \Blackbird\TicketBlaster\Model\Resource\Event\
Collection
     */
public function getEvents()
```

```
        {
    if (!$this->hasData('events')) {
            $events = $this->_eventCollectionFactory
                ->create()
                ->addOrder(
                    EventInterface::CREATION_TIME,
                    EventCollection::SORT_ORDER_DESC
                );
            $this->setData('events', $events);
        }
    return $this->getData('events');
    }


    /**
     * Return identifiers for produced content
     *
     * @return array
     */
    public function getIdentities()
    {
    return [\Blackbird\TicketBlaster\Model\Event::CACHE_TAG . '_' .
    'list'];
    }
}
```

2. Create the `[extension_path]/Block/EventView.php` file and add the following content:

```php
<?php

namespace Blackbird\TicketBlaster\Block;

use Blackbird\TicketBlaster\Api\Data\EventInterface;
use Blackbird\TicketBlaster\Model\Resource\Event\Collection as
EventCollection;
use Magento\Framework\ObjectManagerInterface;

class EventView extends \Magento\Framework\View\Element\Template
implements
    \Magento\Framework\Object\IdentityInterface
{

    /**
     * Construct
     *
```

```
     * @param \Magento\Framework\View\Element\Template\Context
$context
     * @param \Blackbird\TicketBlaster\Model\Event $event
     * @param \Blackbird\TicketBlaster\Model\EventFactory
$eventFactory
     * @param array $data
     */
public function __construct(
        \Magento\Framework\View\Element\Template\Context $context,
        \Blackbird\TicketBlaster\Model\Event $event,
        \Blackbird\TicketBlaster\Model\EventFactory $eventFactory,
array $data = []
    )
    {
        parent::__construct($context, $data);
        $this->_event = $event;
        $this->_eventFactory = $eventFactory;
    }

    /**
     * @return \Blackbird\TicketBlaster\Model\Event
     */
public function getEvent()
    {
if (!$this->hasData('event')) {
if ($this->getEventId()) {
                /** @var \Blackbird\TicketBlaster\Model\Event
$page */
                $event = $this->_eventFactory->create();
            } else {
                $event = $this->_event;
            }
            $this->setData('event', $event);
        }
return $this->getData('event');
    }

    /**
     * Return identifiers for produced content
     *
     * @return array
     */
public function getIdentities()
    {
```

```
return [\Blackbird\TicketBlaster\Model\Event::CACHE_TAG . '_' .
$this->getEvent()->getId()];
    }

}
```

 These two blocks provide methods to our `.phtml` file: `getEvent()` and `getEvents()`.

3. Create the `[extension_path]/etc/frontend/routes.xml` file and add the following content:

```
<?xml version="1.0"?>
<config xmlns:xsi="http://www.w3.org/2001/XMLSchema-instance" xsi:
noNamespaceSchemaLocation="../../../../../../lib/internal/Magento/
Framework/App/etc/routes.xsd">
<router id="standard">
<route id="events" frontName="events">
<module name="Blackbird_TicketBlaster" />
</route>
</router>
</config>
```

 The file declares the `frontName` for the `frontend` environment and targets our `controller` folder in `TicketBlaster`.

4. Create the `[extension_path]/Controller/View/Index.php` file and add the following content:

```php
<?php

namespace Blackbird\TicketBlaster\Controller\View;

class Index extends \Magento\Framework\App\Action\Action {

    /** @var  \Magento\Framework\View\Result\Page */
protected $resultPageFactory;

    /**
     * @param \Magento\Framework\App\Action\Context $context
     */
public function __construct(\Magento\Framework\App\Action\Context
$context, \Magento\Framework\Controller\Result\ForwardFactory
$resultForwardFactory
```

```
    ) {
        $this->resultForwardFactory = $resultForwardFactory;
        parent::__construct($context);
    }

    /**
     * Event Index, shows a single event
     *
     * @return \Magento\Framework\View\Result\PageFactory
     */
public function execute() {
        $event_id = $this->getRequest()->getParam('event_id',
$this->getRequest()->getParam('id', false));
        /** @var \Blackbird\TicketBlaster\Helper\Event $event_
helper */
        $event_helper = $this->_objectManager->get('Blackbird\
TicketBlaster\Helper\Event');
        $result_page = $event_helper->prepareResultEvent($this,
$event_id);
if (!$result_page) {
            $resultForward = $this->resultForwardFactory-
>create();
return $resultForward->forward('noroute');
        }
return $result_page;
    }

}
```

 These two controllers handle the frontend requests to first get the page ID and its parameters, and then load the event model.

5. Update the `[extension_path]/Helper/Event.php` helper class by adding the following code to it:

```
    /**
     * @var \Blackbird\TicketBlaster\Model\Event
     */
    protected $_event;

    /**
     * @var \Magento\Framework\View\Result\PageFactory
     */
```

```
    protected $resultPageFactory;

    /**
     * Store manager
     *
     * @var \Magento\Store\Model\StoreManagerInterface
     */
    protected $_storeManager;

    /**
     * @var \Magento\Customer\Model\Session
     */
    protected $_customerSession;

    /**
     * Constructor
     *
     * @param \Magento\Framework\App\Helper\Context $context
     * @param \Blackbird\TicketBlaster\Model\Event $event
     * @param \Magento\Framework\View\Result\PageFactory
$resultPageFactory
     * @SuppressWarnings(PHPMD.ExcessiveParameterList)
     */
    public function __construct(
        \Magento\Framework\App\Helper\Context $context,
        \Blackbird\TicketBlaster\Model\Event $event,
        \Magento\Framework\View\Result\PageFactory
$resultPageFactory,
        \Magento\Store\Model\StoreManagerInterface $storeManager,
        \Magento\Customer\Model\Session $customerSession
    )
    {

        $this->_event = $event;
        $this->_storeManager = $storeManager;
        $this->resultPageFactory = $resultPageFactory;
        $this->_customerSession = $customerSession;
        parent::__construct($context);
    }

    /**
     * Return an event from given event id.
     *
```

```
     * @param Action $action
     * @param null $eventId
     * @return \Magento\Framework\View\Result\Page|bool
     */
    public function prepareResultEvent(Action $action, $eventId =
null)
    {
        if(!$this->isLoggedIn())
        {
            return false;
        }
        if ($eventId !== null && $eventId !== $this->_event-
>getId()) {
            $delimiterPosition = strrpos($eventId, '|');
            if ($delimiterPosition) {
                $eventId = substr($eventId, 0,
$delimiterPosition);
            }

            $this->_event->setStoreId($this->_storeManager-
>getStore()->getId());
            if (!$this->_event->load($eventId)) {
                return false;
            }
        }

        if (!$this->_event->getId()) {
            return false;
        }

        /** @var \Magento\Framework\View\Result\Page $resultPage
*/
        $resultPage = $this->resultPageFactory->create();
        // We can add our own custom page handles for layout
easily.
        $resultPage->addHandle('ticketblaster_event_view');

        // This will generate a layout handle like: ticketblaster_
event_view_id_1
```

```
        // giving us a unique handle to target specific event if
we wish to.
        $resultPage->addPageLayoutHandles(['id' => $this->_event-
>getId()]);

        // Magento is event driven after all, let's remember to
dispatch our own, to help people
        // who might want to add additional functionality, or
filter the events somehow!
        $this->_eventManager->dispatch(
            'blackbird_ticketblaster_event_render',
            ['event' => $this->_event, 'controller_action' =>
$action]
        );

        return $resultPage;
    }


    /**
     * Is logged in
     *
     * @return bool
     */
    public function isLoggedIn()
    {
        return $this->_customerSession->isLoggedIn();
    }
```

6. Reload the page we created earlier (`http://MAGENTO_URL/events`). You will see a page with the contents of your template in it:

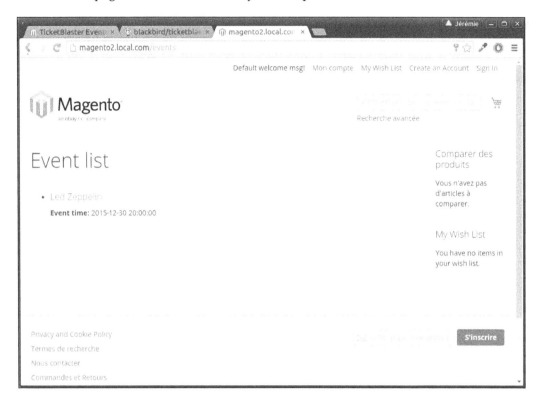

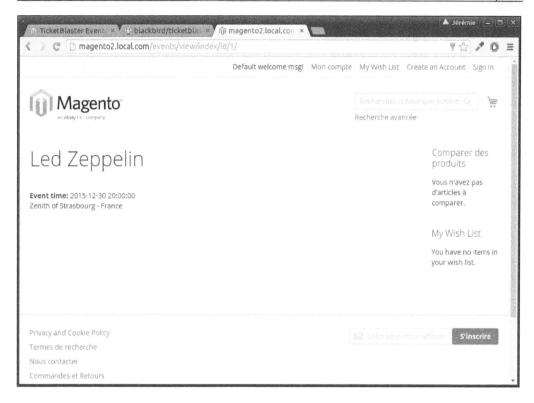

How layouts and templates work

First, the `events_index_index.xml` and `events_view_index.xml` files are automatically loaded, depending on the URL declared earlier in the `etc/frontend/routes.xml` file.

So, in the case of `events_view_index.xml`:

- **events**: The `frontName` XML attribute in the `routes.xml` file
- **view**: The subfolder name in the `Controller` directory
- **index**: The PHP class name for our action created in the previous folder

Finally, the layout declares the correspondence between a block PHP class and a PHTML template file. This association creates the ability of the template to use `$this` as the block PHP class itself.

We can see that the layout is like a conductor, mainly created to distribute roles between frontend files.

Summary

The use of layouts is a very important piece of development with Magento, which adds a lot of possibilities for extending your extension further. You can define new templates and create specific pages as we have done, or override and rewrite core layouts to reorganize Magento pages.

We have seen how to add a complete backend solution to handle our specific needs.

Finally, all our code has been shared on `https://bitbucket.org/` and `https://packagist.org/`, and each update is with comments thanks to Git.

In the next chapter, we will cover more advanced topics, such as custom product types; we will look at a set of best practices for scaling our module in a high-load environment; and we will think about the security of our data.

3
Best Practices and Scaling for the Web

When you create an extension, you must keep in mind that your code will be executed in various environment types, from the smallest website to the biggest businesses on the Web. Your users will be experts, agencies, and people who are new to Magento. That's why you definitely can't provide code that isn't prepared and scaled out for a high-load environment.

Next, we will discuss data security. As a developer, you will know that you can't trust user input; we will see how Magento can help us improve the security of our app.

In this chapter, we will cover the following topics:

- Creating a new product type
- Designing our extension for speed
- Security first

Creating a new product type

As we have seen earlier, tickets should be associated with our events and may even have specific fields and code. Instead of just creating custom attributes, we will create a custom product type specifically for our tickets.

Here's how we do it:

1. Create the [extension_path]/etc/product_types.xml configuration file and add the following code:

```xml
<?xml version="1.0"?>

<configxmlns:xsi="http://www.w3.org/2001/XMLSchema-instance" xsi:n
oNamespaceSchemaLocation="../../Catalog/etc/product_types.xsd">
<type name="ticket" label="Ticket Product"
modelInstance="Blackbird\TicketBlaster\Model\Product\Type\Ticket"
indexPriority="30" sortOrder="30">
<customAttributes>
<attribute name="refundable" value="true"/>
<attribute name="is_real_product" value="false"/>
<attribute name="taxable" value="true"/>
</customAttributes>
</type>
<composableTypes>
<type name="ticket" />
</composableTypes>
</config>
```

This first step is enough for the new product type to appear in the product creation form:

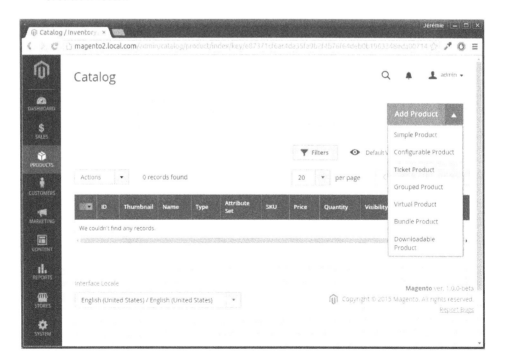

Our new product type will extend the default virtual product of Magento, because we have chosen to only sell virtual products. You can obviously extend simple product types to provide a shipping method, or downloadable types to provide downloads.

2. Create the `[extention_path]/Model/Product/Type` folder.

3. Create the `[extension_path]/Model/Product/Type/Ticket.php` file, as declared in the first step, and add the following code:

```php
<?php

namespace Blackbird\TicketBlaster\Model\Product\Type;

class Ticket extends \Magento\Catalog\Model\Product\Type\Virtual
{

const TYPE_CODE = 'ticket';

public function deleteTypeSpecificData(\Magento\Catalog\Model\
Product $product){


}

}
```

In this step, you can create the product, which will be exactly the same as a virtual product, but without prices (which we will need). The reason for this is that the price attribute isn't applied to the new product type yet.

4. Upgrade your extension version by updating the `[extention_path]/etc/module.xml` file:

```xml
<?xml version="1.0"?>
<configxmlns:xsi="http://www.w3.org/2001/XMLSchema-instance" xsi
:noNamespaceSchemaLocation="../../../../../lib/internal/Magento/
Framework/Module/etc/module.xsd">
<module name="Blackbird_TicketBlaster" setup_version="1.1.0">
<sequence>
<module name="Magento_Catalog"/>
<module name="Blackbird_AnotherModule"/>
</sequence>
</module>
</config>
```

5. Create the `[extension_path]/Setup/InstallData.php` upgrade file and add the following code:

```php
<?php


namespace Blackbird\TicketBlaster\Setup;

use Magento\Eav\Setup\EavSetup;
use Magento\Eav\Setup\EavSetupFactory;
use Magento\Framework\Setup\InstallDataInterface;
use Magento\Framework\Setup\ModuleContextInterface;
use Magento\Framework\Setup\ModuleDataSetupInterface;

classInstallData implements InstallDataInterface
{
    /**
     * EAV setup factory
     *
     * @varEavSetupFactory
     */
    private $eavSetupFactory;

    /**
     * Init
     * @paramEavSetupFactory $eavSetupFactory
     */
    public function __construct(EavSetupFactory $eavSetupFactory)
    {
        $this->eavSetupFactory = $eavSetupFactory;
    }

    public function install(ModuleDataSetupInterface $setup,
ModuleContextInterface $context)
    {
        /** @varEavSetup $eavSetup */
        $eavSetup = $this->eavSetupFactory->create(['setup' =>
$setup]);

        $fieldList = [
            'price',
            'special_price',
            'special_from_date',
            'special_to_date',
            'minimal_price',
```

```
                'cost',
                'tier_price',
                'group_price',
                'tax_class_id',
        ];

        // make these attributes applicable to downloadable
products
foreach ($fieldList as $field) {
            $applyTo = explode(
                ',',
                $eavSetup->getAttribute(\Magento\Catalog\Model\
Product::ENTITY, $field, 'apply_to')
            );
if (!in_array('ticket', $applyTo)) {
                $applyTo[] = 'ticket';
                $eavSetup->updateAttribute(
                    \Magento\Catalog\Model\Product::ENTITY,
                    $field,
                    'apply_to',
implode(',', $applyTo)
                );
        }
    }
    }
}
```

You can see that it is really easy to add installation scripts. We will see how we can use them to upgrade the data and schema of an extension, while adding new functionalities or providing bug fixes to our community of users. They will only have to download the new version of the code and run `bin/Magento` to update it.

Now we have the price available in the product creation form. The next step is to create an attribute destined to make a link to the events.

6. Upgrade your extension version by updating the `[extention_path]/etc/module.xml` file:

```xml
<?xml version="1.0"?>
<configxmlns:xsi="http://www.w3.org/2001/XMLSchema-instance" xsi
:noNamespaceSchemaLocation="../../../../../lib/internal/Magento/
Framework/Module/etc/module.xsd">
```

```
<module name="Blackbird_TicketBlaster" setup_version="1.2.0">
<sequence>
<module name="Magento_Catalog"/>
<module name="Blackbird_AnotherModule"/>
</sequence>
</module>
</config>
```

7. Create the [extension_path]/Setup/UpgradeData.php upgrade file and add the following code:

```php
<?php
/**
 * Copyright © 2015 Magento. All rights reserved.
 * See COPYING.txt for license details.
 */

namespace Blackbird\TicketBlaster\Setup;

use Magento\Eav\Setup\EavSetup;
use Magento\Eav\Setup\EavSetupFactory;
use Magento\Framework\Setup\UpgradeDataInterface;
use Magento\Framework\Setup\ModuleContextInterface;
use Magento\Framework\Setup\ModuleDataSetupInterface;

/**
 * @codeCoverageIgnore
 */
classUpgradeData implements UpgradeDataInterface
{
    /**
     * EAV setup factory
     *
     * @varEavSetupFactory
     */
private $eavSetupFactory;

    /**
     * Init
     *
     * @paramEavSetupFactory $eavSetupFactory
     */
public function __construct(EavSetupFactory $eavSetupFactory)
    {
```

```php
            $this->eavSetupFactory = $eavSetupFactory;
    }


    /**
     * {@inheritdoc}
     * @SuppressWarnings(PHPMD.ExcessiveMethodLength)
     */
public function upgrade(ModuleDataSetupInterface $setup,
ModuleContextInterface $context)
    {

if (version_compare($context->getVersion(), '1.2.0', '<')) {
            /** @varEavSetup $eavSetup */
            $eavSetup = $this->eavSetupFactory->create(['setup' =>
$setup]);

            $eavSetup->addAttribute(
                \Magento\Catalog\Model\Product::ENTITY,
                'event_link',
                [
                    'type' => 'int',
                    'backend' => '',
                    'frontend' => '',
                    'label' => 'Event',
                    'input' => 'select',
                    'class' => '',
                    'source' => 'Blackbird\TicketBlaster\Model\
Event\Attribute\Source\Event',
                    'global' => true,
                    'visible' => true,
                    'required' => true,
                    'user_defined' => true,
                    'default' => '0',
                    'searchable' => false,
                    'filterable' => false,
                    'comparable' => false,
                    'visible_on_front' => false,
                    'unique' => false,
                    'apply_to' => 'ticket',
                    'used_in_product_listing' => 0
                ]
            );
```

```
                // Add the new attribute group
                $eavSetup->addAttributeGroup(\Magento\Catalog\Model\
Product::ENTITY, 'Default', 'TicketBlaster', 2);

                // Update the attribute group by adding our custom
attribute
                $entityTypeId = $eavSetup->getEntityTypeId(\Magento\
Catalog\Model\Product::ENTITY);
                $attributeSetId = $eavSetup->getDefaultAttributeSetId(
$entityTypeId);
                $attributeGroupId = $eavSetup->getAttributeGroupId($en
tityTypeId, $attributeSetId, 'TicketBlaster');

                $eavSetup->addAttributeToGroup(
                    $entityTypeId,
                    $attributeSetId,
                    $attributeGroupId,
                    'event_link',
                    10);
            }
        }
    }
```

This code will add the new attribute, assign it to the default attribute set (called Product Template), and create a group to display it in a separate tab in the product creation form.

The if sequence with the version_compare test permits you to upgrade your extension from one version to another.

The last step defines the source data of this attribute (declared in the source value of the attribute).

8. Create the [extension_path]/Model/Event/Attribute/Source folder.

9. Create the [extension_path]/Model/Event/Attribute/Source/Event. php file and add the following code:

```
<?php

namespace Blackbird\TicketBlaster\Model\Event\Attribute\Source;

class Event extends \Magento\Eav\Model\Entity\Attribute\Source\
Table
{
```

```php
    /**
     * @var \Magento\Store\Model\Resource\Store\CollectionFactory
     */
protected $_eventsFactory;

    /**
     * @param \Magento\Eav\Model\Resource\Entity\Attribute\Option\
CollectionFactory $attrOptionCollectionFactory
     * @param \Magento\Eav\Model\Resource\Entity\Attribute\
OptionFactory $attrOptionFactory
     * @param \Blackbird\TicketBlaster\Model\Resource\Event\
CollectionFactory $eventCollectionFactory,
     */
public function __construct(
        \Magento\Eav\Model\Resource\Entity\Attribute\Option\
CollectionFactory $attrOptionCollectionFactory,
        \Magento\Eav\Model\Resource\Entity\Attribute\OptionFactory
$attrOptionFactory,
        \Blackbird\TicketBlaster\Model\Resource\Event\
CollectionFactory $eventsFactory
    ) {
        parent::__construct($attrOptionCollectionFactory,
$attrOptionFactory);
        $this->_eventsFactory = $eventsFactory;
    }

    /**
     * @return array
     */
public function getAllOptions()
    {
if (!$this->_options) {
            $events = $this->_createEventsCollection();

            $options[] = [
                'label' => '',
                'value' => '',
            ];

foreach($events as $event){
                $options[] = [
                    'label' => $event->getName(),
                    'value' => $event->getId(),
                ];
            }
```

```
            $this->_options = $options;
        }
    return $this->_options;
    }


    /**
     * @return \Magento\Store\Model\Resource\Store\Collection
     */
protected function _createEventsCollection()
    {
    return $this->_eventsFactory->create();
    }
}
```

That's it! We can now launch the `bin/magentosetup:upgrade` command to install the new scripts and try to add a new ticket product:

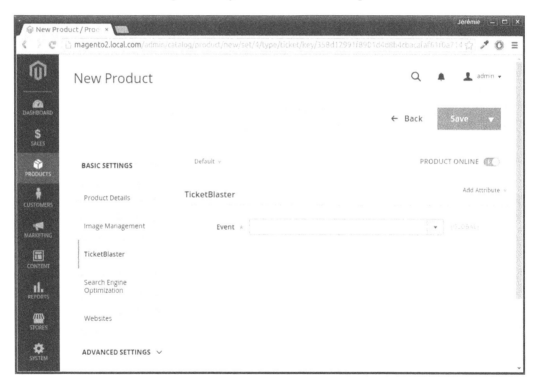

Designing our extension for speed

Magento is a fantastic and high-level platform which works with thousands of files, exchanging a lot of information with databases and generating large HTML pages. Have you ever wondered how this engine generates a page in less than 100 milliseconds?

Magento contains basic tools that help us take care of the consequences of our development. Browser and server tools will be very useful too. We are going to find out about them.

In the second part, we will see that our code can be written in many different ways, but not all render at the same speed.

Enabling developer mode

The developer mode is a mode that forces you to write clean and alert free PHP code the server can generate. This is a good way to prevent performance loss.

The developer mode can be activated through the `.htaccess` file at the root of your Magento installation, or the `pub/` directory if you use it as your document root.

Here's how we go about doing this:

1. Uncomment the following line by removing the # prefix:

    ```
    SetEnv MAGE_MODE developer
    ```

- If you want to enable the developer mode for a specific IP address, replace the line and change it with your IP address in the case of a remote server. Keep the local IP as `127.0.0.1` if you connect to a local Magento installation:
  ```
  SetEnvIf REMOTE_ADDR 127.0.0.1 MAGE_MODE=developer
  ```
- If you want to enable the developer mode for your local copy, and not for the production server, but .htaccess is present in the Git repository, you can limit the mode to the following host name (equivalent to the domain name):
  ```
  SetEnvIf HOST extensions-ticketblaster.local.com
  MAGE_MODE=developer
  ```
- To enable the developer mode in an Nginx installation, add these lines in your `vhost` configuration file:
  ```
  location ~ \.php$ {
  fastcgi_param MAGE_MODE "developer";
  }
  ```

2. To see the developer mode in action, update the `[extension_path]/view/frontend/templates/list.phtml` file by adding the following lines at the beginning of the code:

```php
<?php
echo $test; // Try to display an undefined variable
?>
```

3. Navigate to the `http://MAGENTO_URL/events` page. Magento will output the following error:

Enabling the profiler

The profiler allows you to trace the page request through the code. Additionally, it informs you about page loading and the memory size it consumes.

The profiler can be activated by editing the environment variable in the `<DOCUMENT_ROOT>` /.htaccess file. Add the following line of code:

```
SetEnv MAGE_PROFILER html
```

The MAGE_PROFILER parameter can be set to HTML, CSV file, or Firebug.

- **HTML**: This output format will directly display the profiler at the bottom of the page:

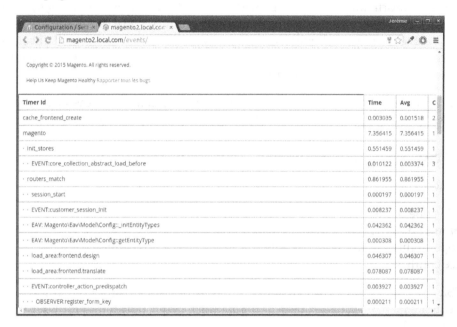

- **CSV file**: This will output the result in the var/log folder
- **Firebug**: This will output the result in the Firebug extension

  The first line of the previous code displays the global page load, followed by the complete path borrowed by the request with your custom *checkpoints* added in the next line:

```
\Magento\Framework\Profiler::start('TEST BLACKBIRD: ' . __
METHOD__, ['group' => 'TEST', 'method' => __METHOD__]);
```

 Read the PHP documentation about memory_get_usage() for more information, at http://php.net/manual/en/function.memory-get-usage.php.

Enabling the debug logs

Magento contains a powerful log system which writes system information and exceptions, and allows you to debug your application more powerfully.

What are logs?

Logs record information. A logger provides a standard mechanism to log system and error logs. These logs record information in chronological order and are used to analyze events and check whether everything is OK or not. Logs help developers find errors and understand how they occurred, or what led to the error. Usually, logs are stored in a local file or a database.

In PHP web applications built using the OOP paradigm, there's generally a logger object to manage logs. In Magento 2, this logger is managed by Monolog.

The PSR-3 standard

Magento 2 complies with the PSR-3 standard. But what's PSR-3?

PSR-3 is one of the different PSR rules. **PSR** is an acronym for **PHP Standard Recommendations**. These recommendations, validated by the PHP Framework Interoperability Group, improve interoperability between frameworks and reduce conflicts.

So, PSR-3 is a Logger interface. Its goal is to write libraries that receive the same `Psr\Log\LoggerInterface` object and guarantee better portability for your solution to other applications.

In **Magento 2**, PSR is located in `<Magento2_Root>/vendor/psr`.

The Monolog library and Magento 2

Magento 2 has a built-in logging facility based on the Monolog library. Monolog is a popular PHP logging solution and is an object-oriented library which is fully extensible, allowing Magento 2 to override and adapt Monolog to its needs. Moreover, Monolog complies with the PSR-3 standard.

If you want to check Monolog and see how it is built, see `<Magento2_Root>/vendor/monolog`.

How Monolog complies with PSR-3

Monolog implements the Logger Interface of the PSR-3 interface and the eight methods according to the levels of the RFC 5424.

In `<Magento2_Root>/app/etc/di.xml`, Magento 2 comes with the following declaration of the implementation:

```
<preference for="Psr\Log\LoggerInterface" type="Magento\Framework\
Logger\Monolog" />
```

This means Magento 2 has a preference for the Logger interface. So each time `Psr\Log\LoggerInterface` is required, an instance of `Magento\Framework\Logger\Monolog` will be supplied. This instance implements the Logger interface. So, PSR-3 coupled with Monolog makes a powerful logging solution that is easy to use.

Channels and handlers

Monolog manages logs using channels that split the logs into different categories. Each channel has a stack of handlers; these handlers can be shared between channels. A channel can be imagined as a type of log, for example debug or system logs. The channel itself does not know how to handle a record and put the message in a log. It delegates this to handlers, which will write records, for example, in files, databases, and so on. So, the main goal for a handler is to write the log records/messages according their levels.

These levels are implemented by `Monolog\Logger` using the levels from `Psr\Log\LoggerInterface`:

```
    /**
     * System is unusable.
     *
     * @param string $message
     * @param array $context
     * @return null
     */
    public function emergency($message, array $context = array());

    /**
     * Action must be taken immediately.
     *
     * Example: Entire website down, database unavailable, etc. This
should
     * trigger the SMS alerts and wake you up.
     *
     * @param string $message
```

```
    * @param array $context
    * @return null
    */
public function alert($message, array $context = array());

    /**
    * Critical conditions.
    *
    * Example: Application component unavailable, unexpected
exception.
    *
    * @param string $message
    * @param array $context
    * @return null
    */
public function critical($message, array $context = array());

    /**
    * Runtime errors that do not require immediate action but should
typically
    * be logged and monitored.
    *
    * @param string $message
    * @param array $context
    * @return null
    */
public function error($message, array $context = array());

    /**
    * Exceptional occurrences that are not errors.
    *
    * Example: Use of deprecated APIs, poor use of an API,
undesirable things
    * that are not necessarily wrong.
    *
    * @param string $message
    * @param array $context
    * @return null
    */
public function warning($message, array $context = array());

    /**
    * Normal but significant events.
    *
```

```
     * @param string $message
     * @param array $context
     * @return null
     */
    public function notice($message, array $context = array());

    /**
     * Interesting events.
     *
     * Example: User logs in, SQL logs.
     *
     * @param string $message
     * @param array $context
     * @return null
     */
    public function info($message, array $context = array());

    /**
     * Detailed debug information.
     *
     * @param string $message
     * @param array $context
     * @return null
     */
    public function debug($message, array $context = array());

    /**
     * Logs with an arbitrary level.
     *
     * @param mixed $level
     * @param string $message
     * @param array $context
     * @return null
     */
    public function log($level, $message, array $context = array());
```

Handlers catch a certain level and write them to the specific log (file, database, mail, and so on). The basic handler is `StreamHandler`, which writes logs in a stream. The log file path is declared in the handler (by default, in `app/logs/`). For example, Magento 2 declared two handlers: `debug` and `system`. In these handlers, the declared `log` file paths are `var/log/debug.log` and `var/log/system.log`.

But how does Magento 2 declare these two handlers and channels?

Let's see this in `<Magento2_Root>/app/etc/di.xml`:

```
<type name="Magento\Framework\Logger\Monolog">
<arguments>
<argument name="name" xsi:type="string">main</argument>
<argument name="handlers"  xsi:type="array">
<item name="system" xsi:type="object">Magento\Framework\Logger\
Handler\System</item>
<item name="debug" xsi:type="object">Magento\Framework\Logger\Handler\
Debug</item>
</argument>
</arguments>
</type>
```

The first argument is the name of the channel; here, the main channel is declared. The second argument is the stack of handlers for this channel; here, there are two handlers declared, handler `system` and handler `debug`. These two objects have a `$fileName` attribute with the path of the `log` file where it will be written, and another attribute, `$loggerType`, which allows the handler to catch all the records of this type.

How to use the Magento 2 logging system

In this section, we will call the different level methods we have seen in the Monolog library part for different levels.

In a model

Create a new file and add the following code to it:

```php
<?php
namespace Blackbird\ticketBlaster\Model\TestModel;

class WriteLog
{
    /**
     * Logging instance
     * @var Extentions\TestLog\Logger\Logger
     */
    protected $_logger;

    /**
     * Constructor
     * @param Extentions\TestLog\Logger\Logger $logger
     */
```

```
    public function __construct(
        \Extentions\TestLog\Logger\Logger $logger
    ) {
        $this->_logger = $logger;
    }

    public function doSomething()
    {
        $this->_logger->notice('This is a notice level');
        $this->_logger->warning('This is a warning level');
        $this->_logger->debug('This is a debug level');
        $this->_logger->info('This is an info level, go to bigbang
!');
    }
}
```

To use the logger in your model, add a \Psr\Log\LoggerInterface object, via a constructor injection, to your $logger attribute so you can use the logger in your methods and write the exception or info in the logs. But you can extend \Magento\ Framework\Model\AbastractModel, which already contains $_logger and many other objects. In this case, there is no need to specify it in the constructor.

In a controller

Using the logger in a controller will be the same as in a model. Your class has received a \Psr\Logger\LoggerInterface object through a constructor injection. But you can get the Logger with the object manager in the controller.

Indeed, your controller extends \Magento\Framework\App\Action\Action, which has an $_objectManager. So, you can call the Logger in the following way:

```
$this->_objectManager->get('Psr\Log\LoggerInterface')->info($e-
>getMessage());
```

In a block

By default, a block extends \Magento\Framework\View\Template, which extends \Magento\Framework\View\Element\AbstractBlock. This abstract class has a $_logger object type of \Psr\Log\LoggerInterface. So, you can use the Logger as you want in your block. Just call $_logger->info($message); or any method described earlier to represent the levels.

How to make your own custom handler and channel

Imagine you want to record special information in a special `log` file, but it does not exist. You will have to write your own handler. You can use it in your own Logger if you decide to create one.

Firstly, let's see how to make our own handler:

1. Create the `[extention_path]/Logger/Handler` directory.

2. Create the `[extention_path]/Logger/Handler/Warning.php` file and add the following code:

```php
<?php

namespace Blackbird\TicketBlaster\Logger\Handler;

use Monolog\Logger;

classWarning extends \Magento\Framework\Logger\Handler\Base
{
    /**
     * Logging level
     * @varint
     */
    protected $loggerType = Logger::WARNING;

    /**
     * File name
     * @var string
     */
    protected $fileName = '/var/log/myCustomWarning.log';
}
```

Here, our handler extends the default handler of Magento 2, `streamHandler`. So your handler will write records in a `log` file. Then, you just have to declare two attributes, `$loggerType` and `$filename`. `$loggerType` defines the type of level your handler will catch, with respect to RFC 5424. All the level types are visible in `\Monolog\Logger`.

Now, we will write a custom logger (channel) extending `\Monolog\Logger`:

3. Create the `[extentions_path]/Logger/Custom.php` file and add the following code:

```php
<?php

namespace Blackbird\TicketBlaster\Logger;
```

```
use Monolog\Logger;

classCustom extends \Magento\Framework\Logger\Monolog
{

}
```

Now we have to register the logger and handler.

4. Edit [extention_path]/etc/di.xml and add the following code before the
    </config> tag:

```
<type name="Blackbird\TicketBlaster\Logger\Handler">
<arguments>
<argument name="filesystem" xsi:type="object">Magento\Framework\
Filesystem\Driver\File</argument>
</arguments>
</type>

<type name="Blackbird\TicketBlaster\Logger\Custom">
<arguments>
<argument name="name" xsi:type="string">myLoggerName</argument>
<argument name="handlers"  xsi:type="array">
<!-- emergency -->
<!-- alert -->
<!-- critical -->
<!-- error -->
<!-- warning --><item name="warning" xsi:type="object">Blackbird\
TicketBlaster\Logger\Handler\Warning</item>
<!-- notice -->
<!-- info -->
<!-- debug -->
</argument>
</arguments>
</type>
```

The logger (channel) does not know how to handle a record. You will have to
delegate it to your handlers. So, add the handlers in di.xml to the logger as
an item in the handlers argument.

This is not strictly required, but it allows the DI to pass specific arguments
to the constructor. If you do not follow this step, then you need to adjust
the constructor to set the handle.

Warning: The order of the handler items is important! Handlers have to be stacked in the right order by following the order declaration of the RFC 5424 levels; otherwise elements in the wrong order will be ignored.

Now, we can use the logger, for example, in the `Model` class:

1. Edit `[extention_path]/Model/Product/Type/Ticket.php` and update the code with the following:

```php
<?php

namespace Blackbird\TicketBlaster\Model\Product\Type;

class Ticket extends \Magento\Catalog\Model\Product\Type\Virtual
{
    protected $_logger;

    const TYPE_CODE = 'ticket';

    public function __construct(
            \Magento\Catalog\Model\Product\Option
$catalogProductOption,
            \Magento\Eav\Model\Config $eavConfig,
            \Magento\Catalog\Model\Product\Type
$catalogProductType,
            \Magento\Framework\Event\ManagerInterface
$eventManager,
            \Magento\MediaStorage\Helper\File\Storage\Database
$fileStorageDb,
            \Magento\Framework\Filesystem $filesystem,
            \Magento\Framework\Registry $coreRegistry,
            \Blackbird\TicketBlaster\Logger\Custom $logger,
            ProductRepositoryInterface $productRepository
    ) {

        $this->_logger = $logger;
        parent::__construct($catalogProductOption, $eavConfig,
$catalogProductType, $eventManager, $fileStorageDb, $filesystem,
$coreRegistry, $logger, $productRepository);
    }

    public function doSomething(){
        $this->_logger->warning('This is a warning level log');
    }
```

```
    public function deleteTypeSpecificData(\Magento\Catalog\Model\
Product $product){


    }


}
```

Our $logger object is instantiated by the dependency injection.

We have seen how you can add your own log file easily with a new module while respecting PSR-3 and reusing Magento 2's built-in log facility.

Enabling your browser's debug panel

Use and abuse this tool, available on all modern browsers through the *F12* key by default:

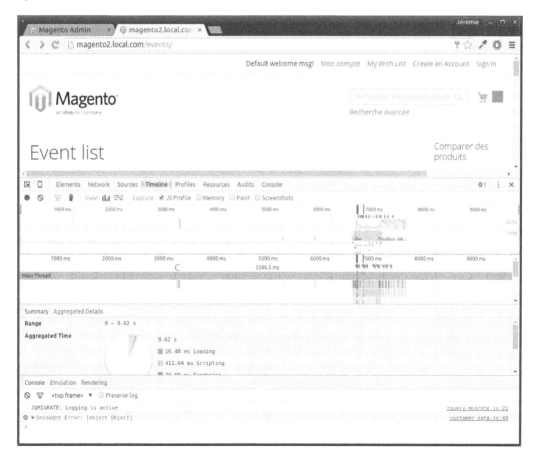

Get the ultimate profiler tool

Try **New Relic**, a powerful software analytics tool which allows you to have complete performance visibility of your software environment. Use this tool, whether during production or for your development:

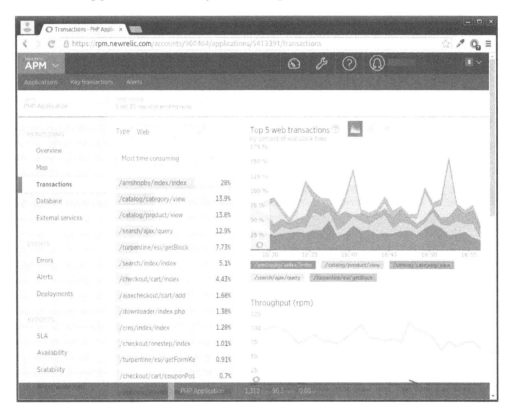

 Visit http://newrelic.com for more information on this solution.

Write clean and efficient code

Now that you have all the necessary tools to measure the performance of your code, you can write better and faster code, ready for a high-load environment.

Don't load any model

Remove the `$this->_event->load($eventId)` calls from your code. This is one of the most memory consuming pieces of code in Magento. But how do we replace this code?

Use collections. They are very powerful and use only a small memory allocation:

```
$events = $this->_eventCollectionFactory
            ->create()
            ->addFieldToSelect(
                'title'
            )
            ->addFieldToSelect(
                'event_id', $eventId
            );
```

Here, `$this->_eventCollectionFactory` is of the `\Blackbird\TicketBlaster\Model\Resource\Event\CollectionFactory` class initialized from our constructor.

See the examples in `app\code\Blackbird\TicketBlaster\Block\EventList.php`.

Getting only really necessary data

After you write the code, look at every unused variable or call and delete them. Use your IDE tools to detect unused code, which helps save time.

Don't write code twice

Yes, I write the methods of an algorithm twice or more if needed. But ask yourself whether Magento already makes it. Use your IDE tools to search for keywords in the Magento code.

Use helpers

Magento's `helper` classes contain utility methods that will allow you to perform common tasks on objects and variables (see *Chapter 1, Introduction to Extension Development*). Most `helper` classes inherit from `\Magento\Framework\App\Helper\AbstractHelper`, which gives you several useful methods by default.

Use layouts

Don't believe the hype; it isn't a good choice to write PHP in order to insert blocks in your templates. Give preference to the use of layouts, as seen in *Chapter 1, Introduction to Extension Development*.

Security first

Security should be considered a part of your code from the very beginning, not added as a layer at the end. The latter approach produces insecure code (tricky patches instead of neat solutions), which may limit functionality and will cost much more (in both time and money).

Five secure coding practices

We will see five secure coding practices that you can follow every day while you develop your extension.

Validate input as strictly as possible

Do not trust all the input parameters, cookie names and values, and HTTP header content (X-Forwarded-For).

Use a lot of Zend_Validate methods. The most common method is pattern validation. Here is an example from the ForgotPasswordPost class of the Magento\ Customer\Controller\Account namespace:

```
if (!\Zend_Validate::is($email, 'EmailAddress')) {
    $this->_getSession()->setForgottenEmail($email);
    $this->messageManager->addError(__('Please correct the email
address.'));
    $resultRedirect->setPath('*/*/forgotpassword');
return $returnRedirect;
}
```

You can validate the attributes' code by using Zend_Validate_Regex. Here is an example of the generateCode($label) from the \Magento\Catalog\Controller\ Adminhtml\Product\Attribute class:

```
$validatorAttrCode = new \Zend_Validate_Regex(['pattern' => '/^[a-z]
[a-z_0-9]{0,29}[a-z0-9]$/']);
if (!$validatorAttrCode->isValid($code)) {
        $code = 'attr_' . ($code ?: substr(md5(time()), 0, 8));
    }
```

Test alphanumeric values as in the `_validateInputRule()` method of the `\Magento\Customer\Model\Metadata\Form\AbstractData` class:

```
$validator = new \Zend_Validate_Alnum(true);
                    $validator->setMessage(__('"%1" invalid type
entered.', $label), \Zend_Validate_Alnum::INVALID);
                    $validator->setMessage(
                        __('"%1" contains non-alphabetic or non-
numeric characters.', $label),
                            \Zend_Validate_Alnum::NOT_ALNUM
                    );
                    $validator->setMessage(__('"%1" is an empty
string.', $label), \Zend_Validate_Alnum::STRING_EMPTY);
if (!$validator->isValid($value)) {
return $validator->getMessages();
                    }
```

Use parameterized queries in your database requests

To prevent using in database requests SQL injection, do not use your variables directly in your requests.

Instead, use one of the following two methods to write your requests.

The first method comes from the `_beforeSave()` method (in the `\Magento\Customer\Model\Resource\Customer` class):

```
$select = $adapter->select()->from(
            $this->getEntityTable(),
            [$this->getEntityIdField()]
    )->where(
            'email = :email'
        );
```

The second comes from `_getLoadRowSelect()` (in the `\Magento\Customer\Model\Resource\Customer` class):

```
$select->where('website_id =?', (int)$object->getWebsiteId());
```

Escape user input

In every default template that uses forms, you can see the use of the `escapeHtml()` method. This is very important; it prevents some **Cross-Site Scripting (XSS)** attacks by executing scripts on the extension's page.

There is only one method to call this method:

```
$this->_escaper->escapeHtml($data);
```

`$this->escaper` has been instanced in the constructor with `\Magento\Framework\Escaper`.

This method will replace every HTML char and tag with a unicode replacement (based on the `htmlspecialchars()` PHP method).

Use synchronized token pattern

In all forms (from Magento 1.7.x onwards), you can see a hidden input that contains a token value:

```php
<?php echo $this->getBlockHtml('formkey'); ?>
```

This code will write a line that is similar to the following:

```
<input name="form_key" type="hidden" value="gUJW0nwlS3a4nn1P" />
```

This value is verified on the server side by Magento when the form is submitted. This protection is very useful against **Cross-Site Request Forgery (CSRF)** attacks and you must use it in all the forms your extension will use.

It is not difficult to check the value of this field, as you can see it at the beginning of almost every controller. Here is the `LoginPost` class from `\Magento\Customer\Account`:

```
if ($this->_getSession()->isLoggedIn() || !$this->formKeyValidator-
>validate($this->getRequest())) {
```

Security headers

There are some headers you can use in your response request:

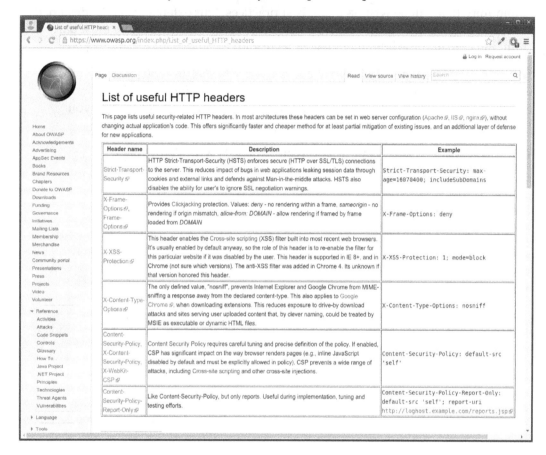

Here is an example from the `arroundDispatch()` method of the `\Magento\PageCacge\Model\App\FrontController\VarnishPlugin` class:

```
$response->setHeader('X-Magento-Debug', 1);
```

 A wide variety of sources exists on the Internet for more information on good security policies, such as www.owasp.org, www.websec.io and other Magento-specific presentations. Do not hesitate to read these other resources.

Summary

After reading this chapter, you should be able to provide an extension to the community that will be written using best practices. Our extension can be designed for speed and we have discovered that the best practices come, for the most part, from Magento and the intelligent use of its resources.

Security comes first; do not forget to check twice whether the code you are writing is secure, by using automatic tests and manual reviews. This aspect is the most important thing to consider today. Your clients and users will not forgive you for not thinking of it!

In the next chapter, we will write complete unit tests with PHPUnit.

4
Magento and Test-driven Development

Our extension has begun to take shape, with more in-depth features. To continue, we will write our first unit test with PHPUnit in order to code a timed checkout associated with the tickets on sale with TicketBlaster.

We also introduce the concept of a sales promotion and make a checkout and an order flow overview, in order to understand how Magento works with these features. By doing this, we will see that our models are fully loaded with the information you can use and we will use rapid methods to discover them. This approach will allow us to implement a special flat rate shipping method in our TicketBlaster extension.

In this chapter, we will cover the following topics:

- Testing in Magento
- Using the Magento Testing Framework
- Writing unit tests with PHPUnit
- Writing a timed checkout

Why perform testing in Magento?

One of the goals of Magento is to improve test automation. These tests are made to improve the quality of the code and to get a serious image in the modern world of software development.

With the number of sensitive Magento projects increasing, test automation is gaining popularity. Magento is delivered with data tests covering all of types of tests, such as unit tests and functional tests. Magento wants to demonstrate the quality and strength of its code, and tests became an integral part of this. So, for Magento, code is incomplete if it has not been tested.

Magento has integrated many tools for testing; PHPUnit is one of them.

Types of test

There are many types of test. Each of these tests has a goal:

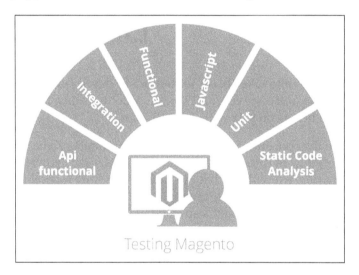

These tests are as follows:

- **Unit tests** are used by developers to isolate the logical parts of code and check whether they work well. They are located in `dev/tests/unit`.

- **Integration tests** determine whether there are issues between components and the environment. These tests are designed to examine many classes in combination. They are located in `dev/tests/integration`.

- **JavaScript tests** check whether the scripts are valid. They are located in `dev/tests/js`.

- **Static Code Analysis tests** analyze the code and check whether it conforms to coding standards or not. They are located in `dev/tests/static`.

- **Functional Tests** are used by developers to find out whether the product's features run correctly. These tests interact with the system as a user. They are located in `dev/tests/functional`.

- **API functional tests** serve the same goal as functional tests, but they are only destined to the API. They are located in `dev/tests/api-functional`.

We are only concerned by unit tests, as these are the most important part of testing.

Magento wants you to provide unit tests with your features. So we will see in the following sections how to use PHPUnit in Magento and how to write unit tests for TicketBlaster. Let's discover the testing in Magento!

Testing in Magento

We are going straight to the core of testing in Magento! Let's see how it is done.

How Magento integrates PHPUnit

Magento offers PHPUnit as a feature for your unit testing development. This tool is a programmer-oriented testing framework based on the xUnit architecture for unit testing frameworks. Magento installed PHPUnit with a composer in `[magento_root]/vendor/phpunit`, so you don't have to install PHPUnit yourself.

All of the data tests are located in `[magento_root]/dev/tests`, so Magento placed a `phpunit.xml` file configuration for each type of test.

These configuration files are used by PHPUnit to know how to run each test. For unit tests, the configuration file is located in `[magento_root]/dev/tests/unit`.

Open the `[magento_root]/dev/tests/unit/phpunit.xml` file. You can see the `<testsuite>` tag and many directories listed in it. PHPUnit will browse your Magento file structure and execute, in these directories, all the files suffixed by `Test.php`:

```
<testsuite name="Magento Unit Tests">
<directory suffix="Test.php">../../../app/code/*/*/Test/Unit</
directory>
<directory suffix="Test.php">../../../dev/tools/*/*/Test/Unit</
directory>
<directory suffix="Test.php">../../../dev/tools/*/*/*/Test/Unit</
directory>
<directory suffix="Test.php">../../../lib/internal/*/*/Test/Unit</
directory>
<directory suffix="Test.php">../../../lib/internal/*/*/*/Test/Unit</
directory>
<directory suffix="Test.php">../../../setup/src/*/*/Test/Unit</
directory>
<directory suffix="Test.php">../../../update/app/code/*/*/Test/Unit</
directory>
</testsuite>
```

You can also find some other useful configurations, such as the `<php>` tag, which allows you to configure `php.ini` values such as `date.timezone` and other options:

```
<php>
<ini name="date.timezone" value="America/Los_Angeles"/>
<ini name="xdebug.max_nesting_level" value="200"/>
</php>
```

 If you cannot find `phpunit.xml`, create it from `phpunit.xml.dist`.

Write unit tests with PHPUnit

The first step when you are creating your class test is to extend `\PHPUnit_Framework_TestCase`. Set up your environment with the public `setUp()` method. Put into this method everything that you want to be executed before your tests. In this method, you will create the objects and data you will use for your tests.

Once the test methods have finished running, the public method `tearDown()` is called. In this method, you will clean up all your data and the objects you used for the tests.

In PHPUnit, a test is described by a public method prefixed by the keyword `test`. If your class does not contain any test methods and you try to run a test, it will throw a *No tests found in class* warning and consider it a failure. A test class has to contain at least one test method.

In this method, you will write your assertions and all your logical tests. In the next sections, you will discover assertions, how to add arguments to the tests, how mocks work, and finally, matchers. All of these features will extend the possibilities for the tests, while avoiding most of the environments.

Assertions

An assertion is a check for the result we are waiting for. If an assertion is not satisfied, the test will be considered to have failed. PHPUnit offers a lot of assert functions in order to give a lot of choices for (in)equality tests.

Some of these are more common than others:

Assertions	Function
AssertTrue(bool $cond)	Check the input to verify that it equals true/false
AssertEquals($expected, $actual)	Check the result against another input for a match
AssertGreaterThan($expected, $actual)	Check the result to see if it's larger than a value (there's also LessThan, GreaterThanOrEqual, and LessThanOrEqual)
AssertContains($needle, array $haystack)	Check whether the input contains a certain value
AssertInternalType($expected, $actual)	Check whether a variable is of a certain type
AssertNull($variable)	Check whether a variable is null
AssertInstanceOf($expected, $actual)	Check whether a variable is an instance of type
AssertRegExp($pattern, $string)	Check the input against a regular expression

All of these assertions accept a last argument, $message = '', which displays a message if the assertion fails.

A complete list of the 39 assertions in PHPUnit is available at https://phpunit.de/manual/current/en/appendixes.assertions.html.

DataProvider

You can put many arguments to your test methods. PHPUnit will fill them with the DataProvider you have declared in the annotation comment line above your method:

```
/**
 * @covers MyClass::myMethod
 * @dataProvider anAnotherMethod
 */
public function testMyMethod($firstArg, $secondArg) {...}

public function anAnotherMethod() {
```

```
return [
        'firstRound' => ['valueArg1', 'valueArg2'],
        'secondRound' => ['valueArg1', 'valueArg2']
    ];
}
```

The `testMyMethod()` test will be called as many times as there are keys in the provider.

Test Double

Some components are hard to test, because they depend on other components that cannot be used in the test environment. So, we replace these components with components that mimic real objects, for which we can control the return results.

These are called **Mocks**. Mocks are just a type of Test Double. There are many other types of Test Double. They are as follows:

- **Dummy:** This is used to fill a parameter, but is never actually used
- **Fake:** This is an implemented object, but it usually takes a shortcut
- **Stubs:** This provides canned answers to the calls made during the test
- **Mocks:** These are pre-programmed objects with an expectation of special returns

When you create a `Mock` of an object, the object is cloned. The cloned object seems to be exactly the same, but this object is empty. When you create it, you can choose to disable the original constructor or change the return value of the methods. For example, your test needs to call a method of a lambda class. But this class is heavy and you already know what this method should return. So you expect, thanks to mocks, what the method will return when it is called.

How do we create and use stubs and mocks?

There are many ways to create mocks. So, let's start with the most intuitive method. We will create a sample mock and see all the possibilities that exist:

```
Class MyTest extends \PHPUnit_Framework_TestCase
{
public function testMethod()
    {
        $args = ['arg1' => 'value1', 'arg2' => 'value2'];
        $methods = ['methodA', 'methodB'];

        // A classic mock
        $mock1 = $this->getMockBuilder('className')
```

```
                    ->setConstructorArgs($args)
                    ->getMock();

        // A mock totally empty
        $mock2 = $this->getMockBuilder('className')
                    ->disableOriginalConstructor()
                    ->getMock();

        // A mock which we want modify return of methods
        // we should change return of methodA and methodB later
        $mock3 = $this->getMockBuilder('className')
                    ->disableOriginalConstructor($methods)
                    ->setMethods()
                    ->getMock();
    }
}
```

This Mock builder is preferable because it is more intuitive than others. If you read the methods applied to this builder, you will already understand what is being done. Here, we have created the mock in three ways:

- The first is a simple mock that we declared as the real object
- The second is made without its original constructor
- The third specifies which methods will return a special return

The following methods are provided by MockBuilder:

Methods	Functions
getMock()	Creates a mock object using a fluent interface.
getMockForAbstractClass()	Creates a mock object for an abstract class using a fluent interface.
getMockForTrait()	Creates a mock object for a trait using a fluent interface.
setMethods($methods)	Specifies the subset of methods to mock. The default is to mock all of them.
setConstructorArgs(array $args)	Specifies the arguments for the constructor.
setMockClassName($name)	Specifies the name of the mock class.

Methods	Functions
disableOriginalConstructor()	Disables the invocation of the original constructor.
enableOriginalConstructor()	Enables the invocation of the original constructor.
disableOriginalClone()	Disables the invocation of the original clone constructor.
enableOriginalClone()	Enables the invocation of the original clone constructor.
disableAutoload()	Disables the use of class autoloading while creating the mock object.
enableAutoload()	Enables the use of class autoloading while creating the mock object.
disableArgumentCloning()	Disables the cloning of arguments passed to the mocked methods.
enableArgumentCloning()	Enables the cloning of arguments passed to the mocked methods.
enableProxyingToOriginalMethods()	Enables the invocation of the original methods.
disableProxyingToOriginalMethods()	Disables the invocation of the original methods.
setProxyTarget($object)	Sets the proxy target.

These methods allow you to adapt your mock to your needs.

It is possible to create mocks quickly with one method and more than one argument:

```
classMyTest extends \PHPUnit_Framework_TestCase
{
public function testMethod()
    {
        $args = ['arg1' => 'value1', 'arg2' => 'value2'];
        $methods = ['methodA', 'methodB'];

        // A mock normally instantiate which will modify methods
    returns
        $mock1 = $this->getMock('className', $methods, $args);
        // Same as preceding but which has disable original
    constructor
```

```
        $mock2 = $this->getMock('className', $methods, [], '', false);
    }
}
```

Here, we have created two mocks of a `className` object. Here are the details of `getMock`:

Method	Function
`$this->getMock(`	Returns a `mock` object for the specified class.
`$originalClassName,`	Name of the class to be mocked.
`$methods = array(),`	When provided, only the methods whose names are in the array are replaced with a configurable test double. The behavior of the other methods is not changed. Providing `null` means that no methods will be replaced.
`$arguments = array(),`	Parameters to pass to the original class constructor.
`$mockClassName = '',`	The class name for the generated test double class.
`$callOriginalConstructor = true,`	This can be used to disable the call to the original class constructor.
`$callOriginalClone = true,`	This can be used to disable the call to the original class clone constructor.
`$callAutoload = true,`	This can be used to disable `__autoload()` during the generation of the test double class.
`$cloneArguments = false,`	Clone arguments.
`$callOriginalMethods = false`	Call original methods.

Other common mocks for an abstract class are as follows:

`$this->getMockForAbstractClass(`	Returns a `mock` object for the specified abstract class with all the abstract methods of the class mocked. Concrete methods to mock can be specified with the last parameter.
`$originalClassName,`	Name of the class to be mocked.

`$arguments = array(),`	Parameters to pass to the original class constructor.
`$mockClassName = '',`	The class name for the generated test double class.
`$callOriginalConstructor = true,`	This can be used to disable the call to the original class constructor.
`$callOriginalClone = true,`	This can be used to disable the call to the original class clone constructor.
`$callAutoload = true,`	This can be used to disable `__autoload()` during the generation of the test double class.
`$mockedMethods = array(),`	Mocked methods.
`$cloneArguments = false,`	Clone arguments.

You can create `Mocks` for `interface`, `class`, `trait`, and so on.

> Look for the other available methods to create mocks:
> - `getMockForTrait()` returns a `mock` object for the specified trait.
> - `getMockFromWsdl()` returns a `mock` object based on the given WSDL file.

Be careful; `getMockClass()` does not return a mock, but a class name.

The complete documentation is available at `https://phpunit.de/manual/current/en/phpunit-book.html`.

Expectations and matchers

Mocks have many uses. Here, we will see `expectations` and `matchers`. Mocks are able to check whether a method was called an exact number of times to control the entry parameters and modify the return value of the mock's methods.

Matchers

This method will do what you want it to do if the matcher is `true`. If the matcher is never reached, it will throw a warning and your test will be considered to have failed. Many matchers are available that specify the number of invocations. Here's a list of them:

`any()`	This returns a matcher that matches when the method it is evaluated for is executed zero or more times
`never()`	This returns a matcher that matches when the method it is evaluated for is never executed
`atLeastOnce()`	This returns a matcher that matches when the method it is evaluated for is executed at least once
`once()`	This returns a matcher that matches when the method it is evaluated for is executed exactly once
`exactly(int $count)`	This returns a matcher that matches when the method it is evaluated for is executed exactly count times
`at(int $index)`	This returns a matcher that matches when the method it is evaluated for is invoked at the given index, starting with 0

Let's see an example of using a mock, assuming our `State` model has an `inflation` method that calls another method, `doublePrice`:

```
/**
 * @covers State::inflation
 * @covers State::double
 */
public function testInflation()
{
    $m = $this->stateMock;    // our model instantiate in setUp

    $m->expects($this->once())->method('doublePrice');

    $m->inflation();    // doublePrice is called once (test do not
failed)
}
```

The will method

This method will replace the returns of a method. It can be used in two ways.
The first way is done in one step by you stubbing a method call to return another
value, thanks to the next methods provided by the mock:

`willReturn($value)`	This stubs a method call to return a value
`willReturnMap(array $valueMap)`	This stubs a method call to return the value from a map
`willReturnArgument($argumentInd ex)`	This stubs a method call to return one of the arguments
`willReturnCallback($callback)`	This stubs a method call to return a value from a callback
`willReturnSelf()`	This stubs a method call to return a reference to the `stub` object
`willReturnOnConsecutiveCalls(...)`	This stubs a method call to return a list of values in the specified order
`willThrowException(Exception $exception)`	This stubs a method call to throw an exception

The second way is done in two steps. You call the `will` method provided by
the mock and pass it as an argument or a `return` statement, provided by the
`TestCase` instance:

```
$mock->expects($matcher)
    ->method($constraint)
    ->will(PHPUnit_Framework_MockObject_Stub $stub);
```

The stubs provided by `PHPUnit_Framework_MockObject_Stub` are the same as the
ones mentioned earlier:

`returnValue($value)`	This returns a value
`returnValueMaparray($valueMap)`	This returns the value from a map
`returnArgument($argumentIndex)`	This returns one of the arguments
`returnCallback($callback)`	This returns a value from a callback
`returnSelf()`	This returns a reference to the `stub` object
`onConsecutiveCalls(...)`	This returns the list of values in order
`throwException(Exception $exception)`	This throws an exception

The with method

The with() method can take any number of arguments, corresponding to the number of arguments to the method being mocked. These arguments will be checked against the mocked method's arguments. If the constraint is met, it will return true in matches().

The withConsecutive() method can take any number of arrays of arguments depending on the calls you want to test against. Each array is a list of constraints that will be checked against the mocked method's arguments, such as in the with() method. So, the first invocation uses the first group of constraints, the second the next, and so on. If the constraint is met, it will return true in matches().

 Be careful; the call index is increased after each invocation.

The withAnyParameters() method does not take any argument. Each argument of the method being mocked will be allowed. It will return true in matches().

Assume that we are in a test case instance and we have a mock with a lambda method:

```
// We assume our lambda method has 3 arguments, an int, a bool and a
string
// We check if arguments are corresponding to the following
$mock->expects($matcher)
    ->method($constraint)
    ->with($this->greaterThan(0), true, 'my string');
// This is the same thing as preceding, but we can specify many tests
$mock->expects($matcher)
    ->method($constraint)
    ->withConsecutive(
array($this->greaterThan(0), true, 'my string'),
array($this->greaterThan(0), false, 'my another string')
    );
// This will return true forever
$mock->expects($matcher)
    ->method($constraint)
    ->withAnyParameters();
```

Magento Test Framework

Magento has created a framework in order to help you in your unit test development. This framework is the product of PHPUnit coupled with Magento. But what are the new features? That's what we will discover in this section.

The goal of Magento Test Framework is to make the development of unit tests easier. There are some classes that extend PHPUnit and offer some basic methods to improve your development. But there are other classes that directly rely on Magento or add new features for your future tests. Here's a quick overview of Test Framework's features:

Method	Function
Autoloader\ExtensionGeneratorAutoloader	This enables code generation for the undeclared Extension and ExtensionInterface types. These files must be generated, since they are referenced in many interfaces/classes and cannot be mocked easily. For unit tests, these are just empty type definitions.
Block\Adminhtml	The basis of the test cases for adminhtml blocks. This class provides many objects. Check out the source code for more details on the features.
Helper\ObjectManager	The helper class for basic object retrieval, such as blocks, models, and so on. Dependency injection will fill arguments with mocks.
Helper\ProxyTesting	The helper class for testing proxy objects.
Listener\GarbageCleanup	The listener for PHPUnit built-in events that enforces the cleanup of cyclic object references.
Matcher\MethodInvokedAtIndex	This matches the invocations per *method* at *position*. Its different of matcher at() which matches invocations per 'position' at 'method'. It's more understandable to use this new feature.
Utility\XsdValidator	Checks and validates an XML file based on its Xsd schema.
AbstractFactoryTestCase	The base of test cases for an abstract factory. This class provides an objectManager and a testCreate() method.
BaseTestCase	The base of the test case. This class provides objectManager, a Boolean data provider, and a basic function to quickly and easily create simple mocks.

These class namespaces are prefixed by `Magento\Framework\TestFramework\Unit\` and are located in `[magento_root]/lib/internal/Magento/Framework/TestFramework/Unit`.

> Magento does not use a lot of its own testing framework. Only some features seem to be used, such as `ObjectManager` (~600 times), `MethodInvokedAtIndex` (~20 times), `XsdValidator` (~100 times), and a bit of `BaseTestCase` (~30 times).
>
> Complete documentation on MTF is available at `http://devdocs.magento.com/guides/v2.0/mtf/mtf_introduction.html`.

Writing unit tests for TicketBlaster

Unit tests are an integral part of your module in Magento. In this section, we will write tests for our TicketBlaster extension, especially focusing on the `Event` class:

1. Create the `[extension_path]/Test` and `[extension_path]/Test/Unit` folders.

   All of our tests have to be placed in this directory. Here, we have decided to write tests on the `Event` model, so we will perform the following steps:

2. Create the `[extension_path]/Test/Unit/Model` folder.

3. Create the `[extension_path]/Test/Unit/Model/EventTBTest.php` file and add the following code:

```php
<?php

namespace Blackbird\TicketBlaster\Test\Unit\Model;

classEventTBTest extends \PHPUnit_Framework_TestCase
{
    /**
     * @var \Blackbird\TicketBlaster\Model\Event|\PHPUnit_
Framework_MockObject_MockObject
     */
    protected $thisMock;

    /**
     * @var \Magento\Backend\Block\Template\Context
     */
    protected $context;
```

```
    /**
     * @var \Magento\Framework\Event\ManagerInterface|\PHPUnit_
Framework_MockObject_MockObject
     */
protected $eventManagerMock;


    /**
     * @var \Blackbird\TicketBlaster\Model\ResourceModel\Event|\
PHPUnit_Framework_MockObject_MockObject
     */
protected $resourceEventMock;

protected function setUp()
    {
        $objectManager = new \Magento\Framework\TestFramework\
Unit\Helper\ObjectManager($this);
        $this->eventManagerMock = $this->getMockBuilder('Magento\
Framework\Event\ManagerInterface')
        ->disableOriginalConstructor()
        ->getMock();
        $this->context = $objectManager->getObject(
                'Magento\Framework\Model\Context',
                [
                        'eventDispatcher' => $this-
>eventManagerMock
                ]
        );
        $this->resourceEventMock = $this-
>getMockBuilder('Blackbird\TicketBlaster\Model\ResourceModel\
Event')
        ->disableOriginalConstructor()
        ->setMethods(
                [
                        'checkUrlKey'
                ]
        )
        ->getMock();
        $this->thisMock = $this->getMockBuilder('Blackbird\
TicketBlaster\Model\Event')
        ->setConstructorArgs(
                [
                        $this->context,
                        $this->getMockBuilder('Magento\Framework\
Registry')
                        ->disableOriginalConstructor()
```

```
                                ->getMock(),
                                $this->getMockBuilder('\Magento\Framework\
UrlInterface')
                                ->disableOriginalConstructor()
                                ->getMock(),
                                $this->getMockBuilder('Magento\Framework\
Model\ResourceModel\AbstractResource')
                                ->disableOriginalConstructor()
                                ->setMethods(
                                        [
                                                '_construct',
                                                'getConnection',
                                        ]
                                )
                                ->getMockForAbstractClass(),
                                $this->getMockBuilder('Magento\Framework\
Data\Collection\AbstractDb')
                                ->disableOriginalConstructor()
                                ->getMockForAbstractClass(),
                        ]
            )
            ->setMethods(
                    [
                            '_construct',
                            '_getResource',
                            'load',
                    ]
            )
            ->getMock();

        $this->thisMock->expects($this->any())
        ->method('_getResource')
        ->willReturn($this->resourceEventMock);
        $this->thisMock->expects($this->any())
        ->method('load')
        ->willReturnSelf();
    }

    /**
     * @covers \Blackbird\TicketBlaster\Model\Event::checkUrlKey
     */
public function testCheckUrlKey()
    {
        $url_key = 'some_key';
```

```
                    $fetchOneResult = 'some result';

                    $this->resourceEventMock->expects($this->atLeastOnce())
                    ->method('checkUrlKey')
                    ->with($url_key)
                    ->willReturn($fetchOneResult);

                    $this->assertInternalType('string', $this->thisMock-
          >checkUrlKey($url_key));
            }
    }
```

We named the test class `EventTBTest` for only one reason: the `EventTest` class test already exists in Magento. It is preferable to keep the model name alone to easily know the goal of your tests.

Congratulations, you have created your first unit test for a module in Magento!

How to run unit tests

To run your previously written test, enter the following command in your terminal:

cd[magento_root]/dev/tests/unit/

phpunit --filter EventTBTest

> If you want to run all the registered unit tests, just enter the following in the command line:
>
> phpunit

The results are pretty clear and permit you to correct your code if necessary:

```
PHPUnit 4.7.2 by Sebastian Bergmann and contributors.

.

Time: 22.11 seconds, Memory: 550.00Mb

OK (1 test, 2 assertions)
```

Writing a timed checkout

The event is held on a precise date and probably at a precise time, so we cannot sell tickets if the event has already begun. We will write a timed checkout to ensure that the tickets can't be sold after a specific configured time.

Writing a unit test

For this unit test, we need to create a ticket product and link it to an event:

1. Create a new product by choosing the **Ticket Product** type:

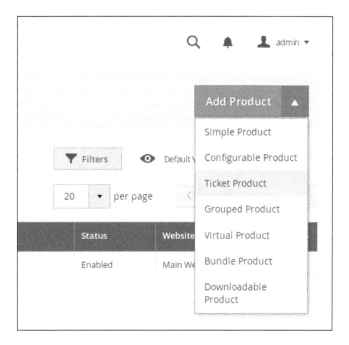

2. Associate this product with an already existing TicketBlaster event:

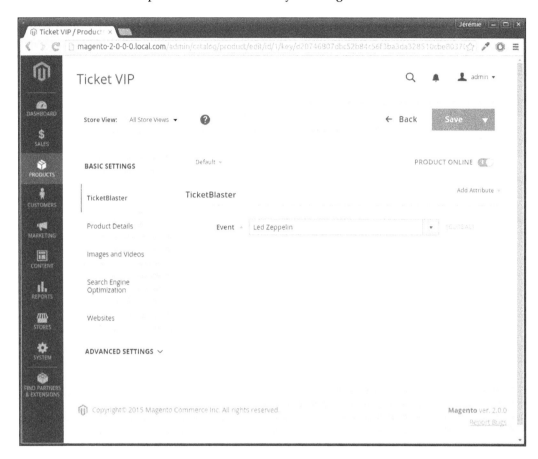

 Do not forget to give a name, description, price, and category, set it to be in stock, and link it to a website.

You should be able to see the product page, as follows:

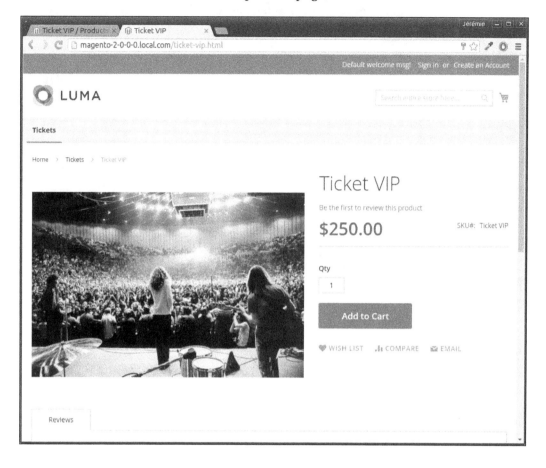

3. Once the product is created, you have to get its identifier back (`entity_id`) by reading it in the product grid in the backend. In my example, the product ID is `907`:

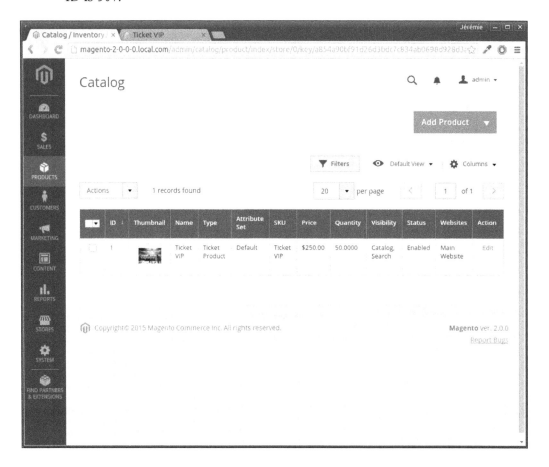

One of the available methods to stop a product being sold is to overload the `\Magento\Catalog\Model\Product\Type\AbstractType::isSalable()` method, because it is called on the product view page, to control the Add **Product** button, and in the checkout process.

This method checks whether the same method exists in a product model.

 Read `isSalable()` from `\Magento\Catalog\Model\Product\Type\AbstractType` to see it.

4. Create the `[extension_path]/Test/Unit/Model/Product/Type` folder.

5. Create `[extension_path]/Test/Unit/Model/Product/Type/NotSalableTest.php` and add the following code:

```php
<?php
namespace Blackbird\TicketBlaster\Test\Unit\Model\Product\Type;

classNotSalableTest extends \PHPUnit_Framework_TestCase
{
    CONST PRODUCT_ID = 1;
protected $_model;
protected $_productObject;
protected $_context;
protected $_eventFactory;
protected $_event;

protected function setUp()
    {
        $objectHelper = new \Magento\Framework\TestFramework\Unit\
Helper\ObjectManager($this);
        $eventManager = $this->getMock('Magento\Framework\Event\
ManagerInterface', [], [], '', false);
        $coreRegistryMock = $this->getMock('Magento\Framework\
Registry', [], [], '', false);
        $fileStorageDbMock = $this->getMock('Magento\MediaStorage\
Helper\File\Storage\Database', [], [], '', false);
        $filesystem = $this->getMockBuilder('Magento\Framework\
Filesystem')
            ->disableOriginalConstructor()
            ->getMock();
        $logger = $this->getMock('Psr\Log\LoggerInterface');
        $productFactoryMock = $this->getMock('Magento\Catalog\
Model\ProductFactory', [], [], '', false);
        $this->_model = $objectHelper->getObject(
            'Magento\Catalog\Model\Product\Type\Virtual',
            [
                'eventManager' => $eventManager,
                'fileStorageDb' => $fileStorageDbMock,
                'filesystem' => $filesystem,
                'coreRegistry' => $coreRegistryMock,
                'logger' => $logger,
                'productFactory' => $productFactoryMock
            ]
        );
```

```
        $objectManager = new \Magento\Framework\TestFramework\
Unit\Helper\ObjectManager($this);
        $this->eventManagerMock = $this->getMockBuilder('Magento\
Framework\Event\ManagerInterface')
        ->disableOriginalConstructor()
        ->getMock();
        $this->context = $objectManager->getObject(
                'Magento\Framework\Model\Context',
                [
                        'eventDispatcher' => $this-
>eventManagerMock
                ]
        );

        $this->_eventFactory = $objectHelper->getObject(
            '\Blackbird\TicketBlaster\Model\EventFactory',
            []
        );

        $this->productObject = $this->_model->load($this->PRODUCT_
ID);

        $this->_event = $this->_eventFactory->create()-
>getCollection()
                ->addFieldToFilter('event_id', $this-
>productObject->getEventLink())
                ->getFirstItem();

    }

    /**
     * @covers \Blackbird\TicketBlaster\Model\Product\
Type::isSalable()
     */
public function testProductIsNotSalable()
    {
        $entity_id = 1;

        $yesterdayDateTime = $context->getLocaleDate()->date()-
>sub(1, Zend_Date::DAY);

        $this->_event->setEventTime($yesterdayDateTime);
        $this->_event->save();
```

```
        $this->assertFalse($this->productObject->isSalable());
    }
}
```

6. Create [magento_root]/Tests/Unit/Model/Product/Type/SalableTest.
   php and add the following code:

```php
<?php
namespace Blackbird\TicketBlaster\Test\Unit\Model\Product\Type;

classNotSalableTest extends \PHPUnit_Framework_TestCase
{
    CONST PRODUCT_ID = 1;
protected $_model;
protected $_productObject;
protected $_context;
protected $_eventFactory;
protected $_event;

protected function setUp()
    {
        $objectHelper = new \Magento\Framework\TestFramework\Unit\
Helper\ObjectManager($this);
        $eventManager = $this->getMock('Magento\Framework\Event\
ManagerInterface', [], [], '', false);
        $coreRegistryMock = $this->getMock('Magento\Framework\
Registry', [], [], '', false);
        $fileStorageDbMock = $this->getMock('Magento\MediaStorage\
Helper\File\Storage\Database', [], [], '', false);
        $filesystem = $this->getMockBuilder('Magento\Framework\
Filesystem')
                ->disableOriginalConstructor()
                ->getMock();
        $logger = $this->getMock('Psr\Log\LoggerInterface');
        $productFactoryMock = $this->getMock('Magento\Catalog\
Model\ProductFactory', [], [], '', false);
        $this->_model = $objectHelper->getObject(
            'Magento\Catalog\Model\Product\Type\Virtual',
            [
                'eventManager' => $eventManager,
                'fileStorageDb' => $fileStorageDbMock,
                'filesystem' => $filesystem,
                'coreRegistry' => $coreRegistryMock,
                'logger' => $logger,
                'productFactory' => $productFactoryMock
```

```
                ]
        );

        $objectManager = new \Magento\Framework\TestFramework\
Unit\Helper\ObjectManager($this);
        $this->eventManagerMock = $this->getMockBuilder('Magento\
Framework\Event\ManagerInterface')
        ->disableOriginalConstructor()
        ->getMock();
        $this->_context = $objectManager->getObject(
                'Magento\Framework\Model\Context',
                [
                        'eventDispatcher' => $this-
>eventManagerMock
                ]
        );

        $this->_eventFactory = $objectHelper->getObject(
            '\Blackbird\TicketBlaster\Model\EventFactory',
            []
        );

        $this->_productObject = $this->_model->loadself::PRODUCT_
ID);

        $this->_event = $this->_eventFactory->create()-
>getCollection()
                ->addFieldToFilter('event_id', $this->_
productObject->getEventLink())
                ->getFirstItem();

    }

    /**
     * @covers \Blackbird\TicketBlaster\Model\Product\
Type::isSalable()
     */
public function testProductIsSalable()
    {
        $entity_id = 1;

        $yesterdayDateTime = $context->getLocaleDate()->date()-
>sub(1, Zend_Date::DAY);
```

```
                $this->_event->setEventTime($yesterdayDateTime);
                $this->_event->save();

                $this->assertTrue($this->productObject->isSalable());
        }
    }
```

 We have to create two separate tests, because each test will create a Magento instance, and this instance uses singletons that don't permit us to change the date of the event and get the new value right now.

7. Launch the two tests one after the other in the `Tests` folder:

```
cd [magento_root]/Tests/Unit/Model/Product/Type
phpunit --filter SalableTest
```

```
PHPUnit 4.7.2 by Sebastian Bergmann and contributors.

.

Time: 1.4 seconds, Memory: 519.00Mb

OK (1 test, 1 assertion)

phpunit --filter NotSalableTest

PHPUnit 4.7.2 by Sebastian Bergmann and contributors.

F

Time: 1.55 seconds, Memory: 520.75Mb

There was 1 failure:

1) \Blackbird\TicketBlaster\Tests\Unit\Model\Product\Type\NotSalab
leTest::testProductIsNotSalable
```

```
Failed asserting that true is false.


FAILURES!

Tests: 1, Assertions: 1, Failures: 1.
```

As we expected, the second test failed. It needs to conform to Test-driven development, so let's implement the functionality!

Writing a timed checkout

We have already created a special TicketBlaster product type (see *Chapter 1, Introduction to Extension Development*) that extends the \Magento\Catalog\Model\Product\Type\AbstractType class. So, we can create the isSalable() method in our \Blackbird\TicketBlaster\Model\Product\Type\Ticket class and it will be called! Perform the following steps

1. Open the [extension_root]/Model/Product/Type/Ticket.php file and add the following code:

```php
<?php

namespace Blackbird\TicketBlaster\Model\Product\Type;

use Magento\Catalog\Api\ProductRepositoryInterface;

class Ticket extends \Magento\Catalog\Model\Product\Type\Virtual
{
    /**
     * Logging instance
     * @varExtentions\TestLog\Logger\Logger
     */
    protected $_logger;
    protected $_event;
    protected $_eventFactory;
    protected $_localeDate;

    const TYPE_CODE = 'ticket';

    public function __construct(
                \Magento\Catalog\Model\Product\Option
    $catalogProductOption,
                \Magento\Eav\Model\Config $eavConfig,
                \Magento\Catalog\Model\Product\Type
    $catalogProductType,
```

```
            \Magento\Framework\Event\ManagerInterface
$eventManager,
            \Magento\MediaStorage\Helper\File\Storage\Database
$fileStorageDb,
            \Magento\Framework\Filesystem $filesystem,
            \Magento\Framework\Registry $coreRegistry,
            \Psr\Log\LoggerInterface $logger,
ProductRepositoryInterface $productRepository,
            \Blackbird\TicketBlaster\Model\EventFactory
$eventFactory,
            \Magento\Framework\View\Element\Context $context
    ) {

        $this->_logger = $logger;
        $this->_eventFactory = $eventFactory;
        $this->_localeDate = $context->getLocaleDate();
        parent::__construct($catalogProductOption, $eavConfig,
$catalogProductType, $eventManager, $fileStorageDb, $filesystem,
$coreRegistry, $logger, $productRepository);
    }

public function doSomething(){
        $this->_logger->warning('This is a warning level log');
    }

public function deleteTypeSpecificData(\Magento\Catalog\Model\
Product $product){

    }

public function isSalable($product)
    {
        $isSalable = parent::isSalable($product);
return ($isSalable&& $this->isEventSalable($product));
    }

public function isEventSalable($product)
    {
        $event = $this->getEvent($product);

        $todayDateTime = $this->_localeDate->date();
        $eventDate = $this->_localeDate->date(strtotime($event-
>getEventTime()));
```

```
    return $todayDateTime< $eventDate;
        }

    public function getEvent($product)
        {
    if(is_null($this->_event)){
                $eventObject = $this->_eventFactory->create();

                $this->_event = $eventObject->getCollection()
                    ->addFieldToFilter('event_id', $product-
>getEventLink())
                    ->getFirstItem();
            }

    return $this->_event;
        }

    }
```

We have overloaded the isSalable() method to add our specific control to
the event. The availability of the event is controlled by isEventSalable(),
which compares today's date with the date of the event.

> In this case, we can also create a special field that the administrator
> can set to a date when the tickets would stop being sold. I used a
> hardcoded example, but you can modify it, obviously.

Finally, the product is saleable only if it is considered saleable by the
Magento checking process, and if the current date is before the date
of the event.

> The isSalable() method is called five times on each product view
> page, so it would be a pity to call the getCollection() method,
> which makes a database request five times. In order to prevent this,
> you can add the $_event property and its getEvent() getter.

2. Create the [extension_root]/view/frontend/layout/catalog_product_
   view.xml file and add the following code:

```xml
<?xml version="1.0"?>
<page layout="1column" xmlns:xsi="http://www.w3.org/2001/
XMLSchema-instance" xsi:noNamespaceSchemaLocation="urn:magento:fra
mework:View/Layout/etc/page_configuration.xsd">
<body>
```

```
<referenceBlock name="product.info.extrahint">
<block class="\Blackbird\TicketBlaster\Block\Catalog\
Product\TimedCheckout" name="ticketblaster.timedcheckout"
template="Blackbird_TicketBlaster::product/view/timedcheckout.
phtml" />
</referenceBlock>
</body>
</page>
```

We declare a new block type and a new template, which are displayed in the extrahint div of the product view page.

3. Create [extension_path]/Block/Catalog/Product/TimedCheckout.php and add the following code:

```
<?php
namespace Blackbird\TicketBlaster\Block\Catalog\Product;

use \Magento\Catalog\Block\Product\View;

classTimedCheckout extends View
{
public function displayTimedCheckoutMessage()
    {
return !$this->getProduct()->isSalable();
    }
}
```

This code sets a method that will be used in the template file to control whether the message can be displayed.

4. Create the [extension_root]/view/frontend/templates/view/timedcheckout.phtml file and add the following code:

```
<?php /** @var $block \Blackbird\TicketBlaster\Block\Catalog\
Product\TimedCheckout */ ?>

<?php if ($block->displayTimedCheckoutMessage()): ?>

<div><p><strong>The event began</strong> : the ticket is no
anymore for sale !</p></div>
<br />
<?phpendif;?>
```

Executing the unit test

To follow TDD, we have to launch a new time for the previously failed tests again:

`phpunitSalableTest`

PHPUnit 4.7.2 by Sebastian Bergmann and contributors.

.

Time: 1.4 seconds, Memory: 289.00Mb

OK (1 test, 1 assertion)

`phpunitNotSalableTest`

PHPUnit 4.7.2 by Sebastian Bergmann and contributors.

.

Time: 1.49 seconds, Memory: 359.00Mb

OK (1 test, 1 assertion)

Our tests passed; the objective has been achieved. We can see the modifications in action on the frontend product page:

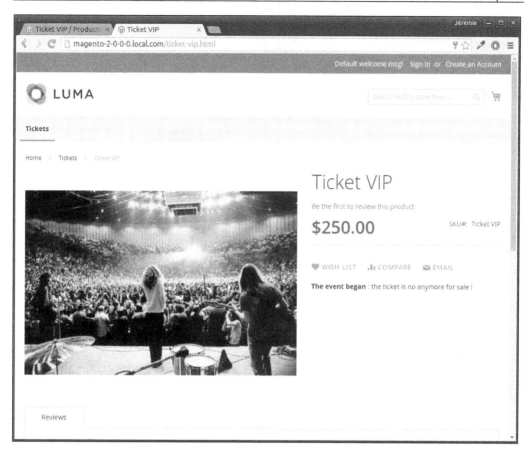

Summary

Magento wants to be perfect; it uses a specialist software approach to achieve this. Therefore, unit tests take up a large part of extension development. For testing, Magento uses PHPUnit, which is a powerful tool and provides many features for tests.

These unit tests are extremely useful for refactoring and regression testing code. They will improve the quality of your codebase in the long run too, and I encourage you to write a lot of tests!

In the following chapter, we will look at internationalization. We will localize our modules for locale-specific languages and currencies.

5
Internationalization

We previously created event models and we can now create new events in the **Admin** panel with customized contents. However, we did not consider multiple stores or multiple languages at that time.

As I mentioned in the last chapter, we will now localize our module for locale-specific languages and currencies. In this chapter, we will see how to handle this aspect of our extension and how it is handled in a complex extension using an EAV table structure.

In this chapter, we will cover the following topics:

- The EAV approach
- Store relation table
- Difference between guests' and registered users' interfaces
- Translation of template interface texts

The EAV approach

The EAV structure in Magento is used for complex models, such as customer and product entities. In our extension, if we want to add a new field for our events, we would have to add a new column in the main table. With the EAV structure, each attribute is stored in a separate table depending on its type. For example, `catalog_product_entity`, `catalog_product_entity_varchar` and `catalog_product_entity_int`.

Each row in the subtables has a foreign key reference to the main table. In order to handle multiple store views in this structure, we will add a column for the store ID in the subtables.

Let's see an example for a product entity, where our main table contains only the main attribute:

The `varchar` table structure is as follows:

The `70` attribute corresponds to the product name and is linked to our `1` entity.

There is a different product name for the store view, `0` (default) and `2` (in French in this example).

In order to create an EAV model, you will have to extend the right class in your code. You can inspire your development on the existing modules, such as customers or products.

Store relation table

In our extension, we will handle the store views scope by using a relation table. This behavior is also used for the CMS pages or blocks, reviews, ratings, and all the models that are not EAV-based and need to be store views-related.

Creating the new table

The first step is to create the new table to store the new data:

1. Create the `[extension_path]/Setup/UpgradeSchema.php` file and add the following code:

```php
<?php

namespace Blackbird\TicketBlaster\Setup;

use Magento\Eav\Setup\EavSetup;
use Magento\Eav\Setup\EavSetupFactory;
use Magento\Framework\Setup\UpgradeSchemaInterface;
```

```
use Magento\Framework\Setup\ModuleContextInterface;
use Magento\Framework\Setup\SchemaSetupInterface;

/**
 * @codeCoverageIgnore
 */
class UpgradeSchema implements UpgradeSchemaInterface
{
    /**
     * EAV setup factory
     *
     * @varEavSetupFactory
     */
    private $eavSetupFactory;

    /**
     * Init
     *
     * @paramEavSetupFactory $eavSetupFactory
     */
    public function __construct(EavSetupFactory $eavSetupFactory)
    {
        $this->eavSetupFactory = $eavSetupFactory;
    }


    public function upgrade(SchemaSetupInterface $setup,
ModuleContextInterface $context)
    {

        if (version_compare($context->getVersion(), '1.3.0', '<'))
{
            $installer = $setup;
            $installer->startSetup();

            /**
             * Create table 'blackbird_ticketblaster_event_store'
             */
            $table = $installer->getConnection()->newTable(
                $installer->getTable('blackbird_ticketblaster_
event_store')
            )->addColumn(
                'event_id',
\Magento\Framework\DB\Ddl\Table::TYPE_SMALLINT,
```

```
                        null,
                        ['nullable' => false, 'primary' => true],
                        'Event ID'
                )->addColumn(
                        'store_id',
        \Magento\Framework\DB\Ddl\Table::TYPE_SMALLINT,
                        null,
                        ['unsigned' => true, 'nullable' => false,
        'primary' => true],
                        'Store ID'
                )->addIndex(
                        $installer->getIdxName('blackbird_ticketblaster_
        event_store', ['store_id']),
                        ['store_id']
                )->addForeignKey(
                        $installer->getFkName('blackbird_ticketblaster_
        event_store', 'event_id', 'blackbird_ticketblaster_event', 'event_
        id'),
                        'event_id',
                        $installer->getTable('blackbird_ticketblaster_
        event'),
                        'event_id',
        \Magento\Framework\DB\Ddl\Table::ACTION_CASCADE
                )->addForeignKey(
                        $installer->getFkName('blackbird_ticketblaster_
        event_store', 'store_id', 'store', 'store_id'),
                        'store_id',
                        $installer->getTable('store'),
                        'store_id',
        \Magento\Framework\DB\Ddl\Table::ACTION_CASCADE
                )->setComment(
                        'TicketBlaster Event To Store Linkage Table'
                );
                $installer->getConnection()->createTable($table);

                $installer->endSetup();
            }
        }
    }
```

The `upgrade` method will handle all the necessary updates in our database for our extension. In order to differentiate the update for a different version of the extension, we surround the script with a `version_compare()` condition.

Once this code is set, we need to tell Magento that our extension has new database upgrades to process.

2. Open the `[extension_path]/etc/module.xml` file and change the version number `1.2.0` to `1.3.0`:

    ```
    <?xml version="1.0"?>
    <configxmlns:xsi="http://www.w3.org/2001/XMLSchema-instance" xsi
    :noNamespaceSchemaLocation="../../../../../lib/internal/Magento/
    Framework/Module/etc/module.xsd">
    <module name="Blackbird_TicketBlaster" setup_version="1.3.0">
    <sequence>
    <module name="Magento_Catalog"/>
    <module name="Blackbird_AnotherModule"/>
    </sequence>
    </module>
    </config>
    ```

3. In your terminal, run the upgrade by typing the following command:

    php bin/magentosetup:upgrade

    The new table structure now contains two columns: `event_id` and `store_id`. This table will store which events are available for store views:

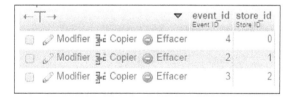

 If you have previously created events, we recommend emptying the existing `blackbird_ticketblaster_event` table, because they won't have a default store view and this may trigger an error output.

Adding the new input to the edit form

In order to select the store view for the content, we will need to add the new input to the edit form. Before running this code, you should add a new store view:

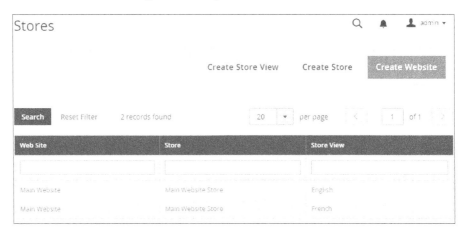

Here's how to do that. Open the `[extension_path]/Block/Adminhtml/Event/Edit/Form.php` file and add the following code in the `_prepareForm()` method, below the last `addField()` call:

```
/* Check if single store mode */
        if (!$this->_storeManager->isSingleStoreMode()) {
            $field = $fieldset->addField(
                'store_id',
                'multiselect',
                [
                    'name' => 'stores[]',
                    'label' => __('Store View'),
                    'title' => __('Store View'),
                    'required' => true,
                    'values' => $this->_systemStore-
>getStoreValuesForForm(false, true)
                ]
            );
            $renderer = $this->getLayout()->createBlock(
                'Magento\Backend\Block\Store\Switcher\Form\Renderer\
Fieldset\Element'
                );
```

```
            $field->setRenderer($renderer);
        } else {
            $fieldset->addField(
                'store_id',
                'hidden',
                ['name' => 'stores[]', 'value' => $this->_
    storeManager->getStore(true)->getId()]
            );
            $model->setStoreId($this->_storeManager->getStore(true)-
    >getId());
        }
```

This results in a new `multiselect` field in the form.

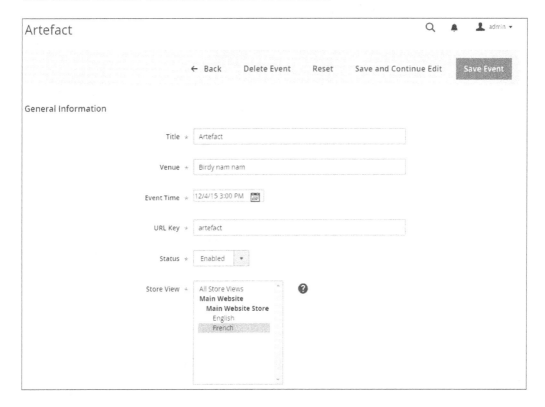

Saving the new data in the new table

Now we have the form and the database table, we have to write the code to save the data from the form:

1. Open the `[extension_path]/Model/Event.php` file and add the following method at its end:

```
/**
    * Receive page store ids
    *
    * @return int[]
    */
   public function getStores()
   {
       return $this->hasData('stores') ? $this->getData('stores')
: $this->getData('store_id');
   }
```

2. Open the `[extension_path]/Model/ResourceModel/Event.php` file and replace all the code with the following code:

```
<?php

namespace Blackbird\TicketBlaster\Model\ResourceModel;

class Event extends \Magento\Framework\Model\ResourceModel\Db\
AbstractDb
{

[...]
```

> The source code can be found in the by-chapter branch of the Git repository, in the Chapter5 folder.

3. The `afterSave()` method is handling our insert queries in the new table. The `afterload()` and `getLoadSelect()` methods are handling the new load mode to select the right events.

4. Your new table is now filled when you save your events; they are also properly loaded when you go back to your edit form.

Showing the store views in the admin grid

In order to inform admin users of the selected store views for one event, we will add a new column in the admin grid:

1. Open the `[extension_path]/Model/ResourceModel/Event/Collection.php` file and replace all the code with the following code:

    ```php
    <?php

    namespace Blackbird\TicketBlaster\Model\ResourceModel\Event;

    class Collection extends \Magento\Framework\Model\ResourceModel\
    Db\Collection\AbstractCollection
    {

    [...]
    ```

 The source code can be found in the by-chapter branch of the Git repository, in the Chapter5 folder.

2. Open the `[extention_path]/view/adminhtml/ui_component/ticketblaster_event_listing.xml` file and add the following XML instructions before the end of the `</filters>` tag:

    ```xml
    <filterSelect name="store_id">
    <argument name="optionsProvider" xsi:type="configurableObject">
    <argument name="class" xsi:type="string">Magento\Cms\Ui\Component\
    Listing\Column\Cms\Options</argument>
    </argument>
    <argument name="data" xsi:type="array">
    <item name="config" xsi:type="array">
    <item name="dataScope" xsi:type="string">store_id</item>
    <item name="label" xsi:type="string" translate="true">Store View</
    item>
    <item name="captionValue" xsi:type="string">0</item>
    </item>
    </argument>
    </filterSelect>
    ```

3. Before the `actionsColumn` tag, add the new column:

    ```xml
    <column name="store_id" class="Magento\Store\Ui\Component\Listing\
    Column\Store">
    <argument name="data" xsi:type="array">
    ```

```
<item name="config" xsi:type="array">
<item name="bodyTmpl" xsi:type="string">ui/grid/cells/html</item>
<item name="sortable" xsi:type="boolean">false</item>
<item name="label" xsi:type="string" translate="true">Store View</
item>
</item>
</argument>
</column>
```

4. You can refresh your grid page and see the new column added at the end.

Magento remembers the previous column's order. If you add a new column, it will always be added at the end of the table. You will have to manually reorder them by dragging and dropping them.

Modifying the frontend event list

Our frontend list (/events) is still listing all the events. In order to list only the events available for our current store view, we need to change a file:

1. Edit the [extension_path]/Block/EventList.php file and replace the code with the following code:

```php
<?php
namespace Blackbird\TicketBlaster\Block;
use Blackbird\TicketBlaster\Api\Data\EventInterface;
use Blackbird\TicketBlaster\Model\ResourceModel\Event\Collection
as EventCollection;
use Magento\Customer\Model\Context;

class EventList extends \Magento\Framework\View\Element\Template
implements \Magento\Framework\DataObject\IdentityInterface
{

    /**
     * Store manager
     *
     * @var \Magento\Store\Model\StoreManagerInterface
     */
    protected $_storeManager;

    /**
     * @var \Magento\Customer\Model\Session
     */
```

```php
    protected $_customerSession;

    /**
     * Construct
     *
     * @param \Magento\Framework\View\Element\Template\Context
$context
     * @param \Blackbird\TicketBlaster\Model\ResourceModel\Event\
CollectionFactory $eventCollectionFactory,
     * @param array $data
     */
    public function __construct(
        \Magento\Framework\View\Element\Template\Context $context,
        \Blackbird\TicketBlaster\Model\ResourceModel\Event\
CollectionFactory $eventCollectionFactory,
        \Magento\Store\Model\StoreManagerInterface $storeManager,
        \Magento\Customer\Model\Session $customerSession,
        array $data = []
    ) {
parent::__construct($context, $data);
        $this->_storeManager = $storeManager;
        $this->_eventCollectionFactory = $eventCollectionFactory;
        $this->_customerSession = $customerSession;
    }

    /**
     * @return \Blackbird\TicketBlaster\Model\ResourceModel\Event\
Collection
     */
    public function getEvents()
    {
        if (!$this->hasData('events')) {
            $events = $this->_eventCollectionFactory
                ->create()
                ->addOrder(
EventInterface::CREATION_TIME,
EventCollection::SORT_ORDER_DESC
                )
                ->addStoreFilter($this->_storeManager->getStore()-
>getId());
            $this->setData('events', $events);
        }
        return $this->getData('events');
    }
```

```
/**
 * Return identifiers for produced content
 *
 * @return array
 */
public function getIdentities()
{
    return [\Blackbird\TicketBlaster\Model\Event::CACHE_TAG .
'_' . 'list'];
}

/**
 * Is logged in
 *
 * @return bool
 */
public function isLoggedIn()
{
    return $this->_customerSession->isLoggedIn();
}
}
```

2. Note that we have a new property available and instantiated in our constructor: `storeManager`. Thanks to this class, we can filter our collection with the store view ID by calling the `addStoreFilter()` method on our events collection.

Restricting the frontend access by store view

The events will not be listed in our list page if they are not available for the current store view, but they can still be accessed with their direct URL, for example `http://[magento_url]/events/view/index/event_id/2`.

We will change this to restrict the frontend access by store view:

1. Open the `[extention_path]/Helper/Event.php` file and replace the code with the following code:

```php
<?php

namespace Blackbird\TicketBlaster\Helper;

use Blackbird\TicketBlaster\Api\Data\EventInterface;
use Blackbird\TicketBlaster\Model\ResourceModel\Event\Collection
as EventCollection;
```

```
use Magento\Framework\App\Action\Action;

class Event extends \Magento\Framework\App\Helper\AbstractHelper
{

    /**
     * @var \Blackbird\TicketBlaster\Model\Event
     */
    protected $_event;

    /**
     * @var \Magento\Framework\View\Result\PageFactory
     */
    protected $resultPageFactory;

    /**
     * Store manager
     *
     * @var \Magento\Store\Model\StoreManagerInterface
     */
    protected $_storeManager;

    /**
     * Constructor
     *
     * @param \Magento\Framework\App\Helper\Context $context
     * @param \Blackbird\TicketBlaster\Model\Event $event
     * @param \Magento\Framework\View\Result\PageFactory
$resultPageFactory
     * @SuppressWarnings(PHPMD.ExcessiveParameterList)
     */
    public function __construct(
        \Magento\Framework\App\Helper\Context $context,
        \Blackbird\TicketBlaster\Model\Event $event,
        \Magento\Framework\View\Result\PageFactory
$resultPageFactory,
        \Magento\Store\Model\StoreManagerInterface $storeManager,
    )
    {
        $this->_event = $event;
        $this->_storeManager = $storeManager;
        $this->resultPageFactory = $resultPageFactory;
        $this->_customerSession = $customerSession;
parent::__construct($context);
```

```
        }

        /**
         * Return an event from given event id.
         *
         * @param Action $action
         * @param null $eventId
         * @return \Magento\Framework\View\Result\Page|bool
         */
        public function prepareResultEvent(Action $action, $eventId =
null)
        {
            if ($eventId !== null && $eventId !== $this->_event-
>getId()) {
                $delimiterPosition = strrpos($eventId, '|');
                if ($delimiterPosition) {
                    $eventId = substr($eventId, 0,
$delimiterPosition);
                }

                $this->_event->setStoreId($this->_storeManager-
>getStore()->getId());
                if (!$this->_event->load($eventId)) {
                    return false;
                }
            }

            if (!$this->_event->getId()) {
                return false;
            }

            /** @var \Magento\Framework\View\Result\Page $resultPage
*/
            $resultPage = $this->resultPageFactory->create();
            // We can add our own custom page handles for layout
easily.
            $resultPage->addHandle('ticketblaster_event_view');

            // This will generate a layout handle like: ticketblaster_
event_view_id_1
            // giving us a unique handle to target specific event if
we wish to.
            $resultPage->addPageLayoutHandles(['id' => $this->_event-
>getId()]);
```

```
        // Magento is event driven after all, lets remember to
dispatch our own, to help people
        // who might want to add additional functionality, or
filter the events somehow!
        $this->_eventManager->dispatch(
            'blackbird_ticketblaster_event_render',
            ['event' => $this->_event, 'controller_action' =>
$action]
        );

        return $resultPage;
    }
}
```

2. The `setStoreId()` method called on our model will load the model only for the given ID. The events are no longer available through their direct URL if we are not on their available store view.

Differentiating the guests and registered users' interface

In this section, we will see how to restrict the frontend features for guest users. In our example, the objective is to restrict access to the **Details** page for logged out users.

Adding the isLoggedIn() method

First of all, we need to add a new method in our block, which will define whether the user is logged in or not:

1. Open the `[extension_path]/Block/EventList.php` file and add a new attribute:

   ```
   protected $_customerSession;
   ```

2. Instantiate this new attribute in the constructor:

   ```
   public function __construct(
           \Magento\Framework\View\Element\Template\Context $context,
           \Blackbird\TicketBlaster\Model\ResourceModel\Event\
   CollectionFactory $eventCollectionFactory,
           \Magento\Store\Model\StoreManagerInterface $storeManager,
           \Magento\Customer\Model\Session $customerSession,
           array $data = []
       ) {
   ```

```
parent::__construct($context, $data);
        $this->_storeManager = $storeManager;
        $this->_eventCollectionFactory = $eventCollectionFactory;
        $this->_customerSession = $customerSession;
}
```

3. Finally, use this model to create our method:

```
/**
 * Is logged in
 *
 * @return bool
 */
public function isLoggedIn()
{
    return $this->_customerSession->isLoggedIn();
}
```

Restricting access in the template file

Here's how you can restrict access in the template file:

1. Open the `[extension_path]/view/frontend/templates/list.phtml` file and add the necessary restrictions:

```
<?php /** @var $block \Blackbird\TicketBlaster\Block\EventList */
?>
<h1><?php echo __('Event list') ?></h1>

<ul class="ticketblaster-events-list">

<?php /** @var $event \Blackbird\TicketBlaster\Model\Event */ ?>
<?phpforeach ($block->getEvents() as $event): ?>
<li class="ticketblaster-event-list-item">
<h3 class="ticketblaster-event-item-title">
<?php if($block->isLoggedIn()): ?>
<a href="<?php echo $event->getUrl() ?>"><?php echo $event-
>getTitle() ?></a>
<?php else: ?>
<?php echo $event->getTitle() ?>
<?phpendif; ?>
</h3>

<div class="ticketblaster-event-item-content">
<?php echo $event->getContent(); ?>
</div>
```

```
<div class="ticketblaster-event-item-meta">
<strong><?php echo __('Event time:') ?></strong><?php echo $event-
>getEventTime() ?>
</div>

<?php if($block->isLoggedIn()): ?>
<div class="ticketblaster-event-readmore">
<a href="<?php echo $event->getUrl() ?>">&raquo; <?php echo __
('Read more') ?></a>
</div>
<?php else: ?>
<div class="ticketblaster-event-readmore">
<i><?php echo __('Please sign in to read more details.'); ?></i>
</div>
<?phpendif; ?>
</li>
<?phpendforeach; ?>

</ul>
```

2. We call our method using `$block->isLoggedIn()` and wrap the HTML with conditions.

Restricting direct access to the Details page

We cannot see the **Details** page links in our list anymore. However, it is still possible to access them with their direct URL: `http://[magento_url]/events/view/index/event_id/1`. The following steps show you how to restrict direct access to the **Details** page:

1. Open the `[extension_path]/Helper/Event.php` file.

2. Add the following property before the constructor:

    ```
    /**
     * @var \Magento\Customer\Model\Session
     */
    protected $_customerSession;
    ```

3. Add the following argument in the constructor arguments list:

    ```
    \Magento\Customer\Model\Session $customerSession
    ```

4. Add the following code at the beginning of the `prepareResultEvent()` method:

```
if(!$this->isLoggedIn())
{
    return false;
}
```

5. Finally, add the following method at the end of the class:

```
/**
 * Is logged in
 *
 * @return bool
 */
public function isLoggedIn()
{
    return $this->_customerSession->isLoggedIn();
}
```

In the same way, we will instantiate the model `customerSession` and prevent the page from loading, if needed.

Translation of template interface texts

In order to translate the texts written directly in the template file, for the interface or in your PHP class, you need to use the `__('Your text here')` method. Magento looks for a corresponding match within all the translation CSV files.

There is nothing to be declared in XML; you simply have to create a new folder at the root of your module and create the required CSV:

1. Create the `[extension_path]/i18n` folder.

2. Create `[extension_path]/i18n/en_US.csv` and add the following code:

```
"Event time:","Event time:"
"Please sign in to read more details.","Please sign in to read
more details."
"Read more","Read more"

Create [extension_path]/i18n/en_US.csv and add the following code:

"Event time:","Date de l'évènement :"
"Pleasesign in to read more details.","Merci de vous inscrire pour
plus de détails."
"Read more","Lire la suite"
```

The CSV file contains the correspondences between the key used in the code and the value in its final language.

Translation of e-mail templates: creating and translating the e-mails

We will add a new form in the **Details** page to share the event to a friend. The first step is to declare your e-mail template.

1. To declare your e-mail template, create a new [extension_path]/etc/ email_templates.xml file and add the following code:

```
<?xml version="1.0"?>
<configxmlns:xsi="http://www.w3.org/2001/XMLSchema-instance" xsi:
noNamespaceSchemaLocation="urn:magento:module:Magento_Email:etc/
email_templates.xsd">
<template id="ticketblaster_email_email_template" label="Share
Form" file="share_form.html" type="text" module="Blackbird_
TicketBlaster" area="adminhtml"/>
</config>
```

 This XML line declares a new template ID, label, file path, module, and area (frontend or adminhtml).

2. Next, create the corresponding template by creating the [extension_path]/ view/adminhtml/email/share_form.html file and add the following code:

```
<!--@subject Share Form@-->
<!--@vars {
"varpost.email":"Sharer Email",
"varevent.title":"Event Title",
"varevent.venue":"Event Venue"
} @-->

<p>{{trans "Your friend %email is sharing an event with you:"
email=$post.email}}</p>
{{trans "Title: %title" title=$event.title}}<br/>
{{trans "Venue: %venue" venue=$event.venue}}<br/>

<p>{{trans "View the detailed page: %url" url=$event.url}}</p>
```

Note that in order to translate texts within the HTML file, we use the `trans` function, which works like the default PHP `printf()` function. The function will also use our i18n CSV files to find a match for the text.

 Your e-mail template can also be overridden directly from the backoffice: **Marketing | Email templates**.

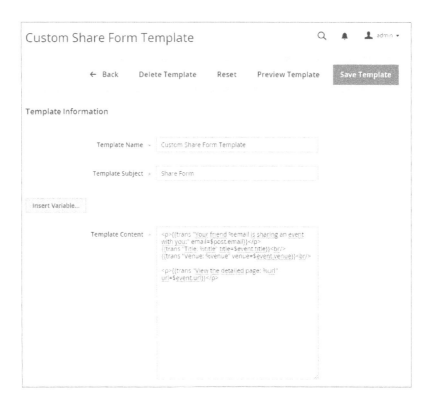

The e-mail template is ready; we will also add the ability to change it in the system configuration and allow users to determine the sender's e-mail and name:

1. Create the `[extension_path]/etc/adminhtml/system.xml` file and add the following code:

```xml
<?xml version="1.0"?>
<configxmlns:xsi="http://www.w3.org/2001/XMLSchema-instance" xsi:
noNamespaceSchemaLocation="urn:magento:module:Magento_Config:etc/
system_file.xsd">
```

```
<system>
<section id="ticketblaster" translate="label" type="text"
sortOrder="100" showInDefault="1" showInWebsite="1"
showInStore="1">
<label>Ticket Blaster</label>
<tab>general</tab>
<resource>Blackbird_TicketBlaster::event</resource>
<group id="email" translate="label" type="text" sortOrder="50"
showInDefault="1" showInWebsite="1" showInStore="1">
<label>Email Options</label>
<field id="recipient_email" translate="label" type="text"
sortOrder="10" showInDefault="1" showInWebsite="1"
showInStore="1">
<label>Send Emails To</label>
<validate>validate-email</validate>
</field>
<field id="sender_email_identity" translate="label"
type="select" sortOrder="20" showInDefault="1" showInWebsite="1"
showInStore="1">
<label>Email Sender</label>
<source_model>Magento\Config\Model\Config\Source\Email\Identity</
source_model>
</field>
<field id="email_template" translate="label comment"
type="select" sortOrder="30" showInDefault="1" showInWebsite="1"
showInStore="1">
<label>Email Template</label>
<comment>Email template chosen based on theme fallback when
"Default" option is selected.</comment>
<source_model>Magento\Config\Model\Config\Source\Email\Template</
source_model>
</field>
</group>
</section>
</system>
</config>
```

2. Create the `[extension_path]/etc/config.xml` file and add the following
   code:

```
<?xml version="1.0"?>
<configxmlns:xsi="http://www.w3.org/2001/XMLSchema-instance" xsi:
noNamespaceSchemaLocation="urn:magento:module:Magento_Store:etc/
config.xsd">
<default>
<ticketblaster>
<email>
```

```
<recipient_email>
<![CDATA[hello@example.com]]>
</recipient_email>
<sender_email_identity>custom2</sender_email_identity>
<email_template>ticketblaster_email_email_template</email_
template>
</email>
</ticketblaster>
</default>
</config>
```

 Thanks to these two files, you can change the configuration for the e-mail template in the **Admin** panel (**Stores | Configuration**).

Let's create our HTML form and the controller that will handle our submission:

1. Open the existing `[extension_path]/view/frontend/templates/view.phtml` file and add the following code at the end:

```
<form action="<?php echo $block->getUrl('events/view/share',
array('event_id' => $event->getId())); ?>" method="post" id="form-
validate" class="form">
<h3>
<?php echo __('Share this event to my friend'); ?>
</h3>
<input type="email" name="email" class="input-text"
placeholder="email" />
<button type="submit" class="button"><?php echo __('Share'); ?></
button>
</form>
```

2. Create the `[extension_path]/Controller/View/Share.php` file and add the following code:

```
<?php

namespace Blackbird\TicketBlaster\Controller\View;

use Magento\Framework\Exception\NotFoundException;
use Magento\Framework\App\RequestInterface;
use Magento\Store\Model\ScopeInterface;
use Blackbird\TicketBlaster\Api\Data\EventInterface;

class Share extends \Magento\Framework\App\Action\Action {

[...]
```

The source code can be found in the by-chapter branch of the Git repository, in the Chapter5 folder.

This controller will get the necessary configuration entirely from the admin and generate the e-mail to be sent.

Testing our code by sending the e-mail

Go to the page of an event and fill in the form we prepared. When you submit it, Magento will send the e-mail immediately.

Summary

In this chapter, we addressed all the main processes that are run for internationalization. We can now create and control the availability of our events with regards to Magento's stores and translate the contents of our pages and e-mails.

In the next chapter, we will see how to optimize TicketBlaster and our code for speed, and how to measure conversion rates.

6
Optimizing for Speed and Measuring Conversion Rates

We previously overviewed and worked with and for internationalization. To make an extension that will be used by many people around the world, we have to write it in the best possible way.

Most Internet shoppers "abandon" a store if it takes longer than 3 seconds to load. This means that we have 3 seconds to surprise and delight our customers. Given this challenge, we will optimize our module based on best practices and look into profiling techniques for identifying potential performance bottlenecks. We will briefly touch upon the topics of frontend development and optimizing our Magento plugins for speedy transfer.

In this chapter, we'll be looking at:

- Performance indicators
- Best practices for optimizing performance
- New Relic

Performance indicators

The loading time of an online store is a key aspect of its success. Many studies have shown the impact of a slow website on conversion rate. According to the **Consumer Response to Travel Site Performance** report from 2010, 57% of online shoppers will wait 3 seconds or less before abandoning a website. This well-known "first 3 seconds to surprise" is probably going to decrease to less than 2 seconds with the rise of high-speed Internet connections. Younger people are even more impatient when they encounter a slow website.

Well, before design or UX considerations, loading speed is the first key characteristic that will keep or lose your potential customers. The Internet user is demanding and even before you display your online shop, half of users visiting a slow online store will leave the website before clicking on the second page. A high **bounce rate** can be even more disastrous if we consider that users give bad feedback to their friends or family, or even on online platforms. The bounce rate also increases the number of users that may potentially go to rival websites and represent a loss of earnings for our shop.

The bounce rate is just one performance indicator among many. Obviously, the key rate for an e-commerce website is the conversion rate. A 1-second delay in page responses can result in a 7% reduction in conversions. For an e-commerce website making $10,000/day, this 1-second delay could potentially cost $250,000 in lost sales every year.

We also need to consider the satisfaction of users. The conversion rate is directly linked to the satisfaction parameter. The higher the loading speed, the lower the user satisfaction score and conversion rate will be.

The **conversion rate** is also affected by a high cart abandonment rate. Indeed, 20% of users abandon their cart because of long loading times. Among 1,568 participants in a survey by Brand Perfect, more than 1,000 said that "slow browsing pages or product images" irritate them most while shopping online. The survey also asked what would improve their experience, and more than half of the responses were "a faster website."

User experience plays a key role in developing customer loyalty: 88% of users stated they wouldn't go back to a store if they consider the website to be too slow.

Slow websites are not SEO-friendly

Speed optimization is frequently a part of SEO issues. Google has been using site speed signals in its search ranking algorithms since 2010. The biggest search engine in the world believes that faster websites create happier users. Their internal study showed that when a website responds slowly, visitors spend less time there. The correlation between the response time of a website and its position in search results is becoming undeniable. The famous "mobile-friendly" philosophy of Google is also to consider loading speed as a key indicator of its page ranking system.

Going further, several tools were proposed by Google to identify and optimize the speed performance of a website:

- Google Analytics and its Real User Monitoring features to monitor the loading speed of your website
- PageSpeed Insights, which allow you to diagnose your performance
- Google WebMaster Tools, which show the access speed of a Google Bot during its crawl on your website

The **pogo-sticking** control of Google is also a determining factor of its algorithm. This indicator calculates the rate of people going back to Google's search results after having clicked on a link. A long loading time will almost certainly push the user to try a different website on the search results page. A high pogo-sticking rate is not necessarily linked to a lack of speed, but a slow website will certainly have a high pogo-sticking rate. It will affect the position of the website on Google's page rank and inevitably decrease the conversion rate of an online store.

Red Slow Label and **Slow To Load** are two tests made by Google to identify slow websites and inform the user before they click on the link. It will advise the user with a label displayed in the search results. These two new features are still works in progress at Google. These experiments again show how important speed is for SEO optimization.

Best practices

If it's not properly configured, Magento will run slowly, since it is a heavy solution. Adding non-optimized extensions will further increase the loading time of your store.

Editing the .htaccess file for compression

Magento has thousands of scripts loading on each server request. You can reduce the loading time by enabling `gzip` compression.

[By default, this option is disabled in Magento.]

To enable `gzip` compression, your server must have the `mod_deflate` module enabled. Then, you need to activate `zlib` output compression as follows.

Open the `[magento_root]/.htaccess` file and modify it by uncommenting the following lines:

```
##############################################
## enable resulting html compression

    php_flag zlib.output_compression on

##############################################
## enable apache served files compression
## http://developer.yahoo.com/performance/rules.html#gzip

    # Insert filter on all content
    SetOutputFilter DEFLATE
    # Insert filter on selected content types only
    AddOutputFilterByType DEFLATE text/html text/plain text/xml text/
css text/javascript

    # Netscape 4.x has some problems...
    BrowserMatch ^Mozilla/4 gzip-only-text/html

    # Netscape 4.06-4.08 have some more problems
    BrowserMatch ^Mozilla/4\.0[678] no-gzip

    # MSIE masquerades as Netscape, but it is fine
    BrowserMatch \bMSIE !no-gzip !gzip-only-text/html

    # Don't compress images
    SetEnvIfNoCase Request_URI \.(?:gif|jpe?g|png)$ no-gzip dont-vary

    # Make sure proxies don't deliver the wrong content
    Header append Vary User-Agent env=!dont-vary
```

Full page cache

The **full page caching** (**FPC**) feature of Magento is a technique used to copy and store output content in a temporary container. For future requests, FPC files will help reduce server load, bandwidth usage, and memory consumption.

Magento integrates **Varnish** for the FPC feature. This solution will generate a unique request for several visitors asking for the same resource. The following figure shows how it works:

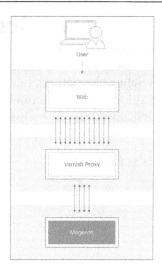

 By default, caching is set to **Built-in Application**. You can enable the Varnish caching system and configure it by navigating to **Stores | Configuration | Advanced | System**.

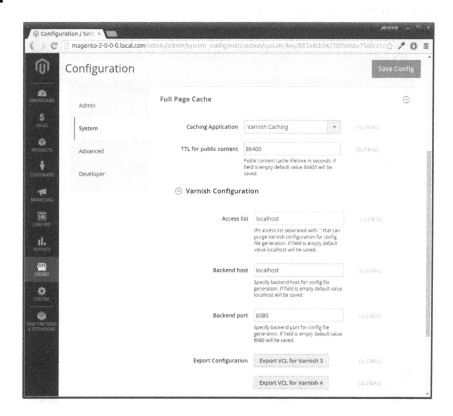

Minify and merge CSS/JavaScript files

The load speed of your Magento extension can be increased by the **minification** of CSS and **JavaScript (JS)** files. This technique will compress your code by deleting useless bytes such as spacing, newline characters, comments, or indentation. It will help you reduce bandwidth consumption and the number of HTTP requests on your server. Reducing file size will speed up the script execution of your extension. Merging JS files will also reduce the number of requests made for each.

Check whether your CSS code is as follows:

```
h1, h2 {
    color:red;
}
p {
    font-family:arial;
}
```

If so, your minified code will look like this:

```
h1,h2{ color:red;}p{font-family:arial;}
```

If you develop a custom theme or an extension with heavy usage of CSS and JS files, it is essential to enable the JS and CSS minify/merge options.

The settings for these are in **STORES** | **Configuration** | **Advanced** | **Developer**:

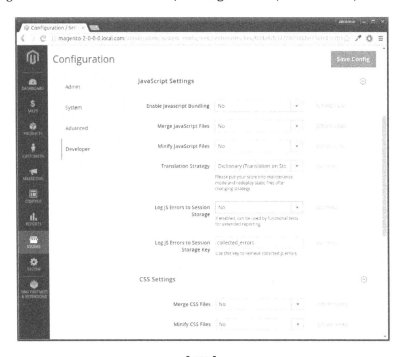

Configuring a CDN server

A **content delivery network (CDN)** is a large, distributed system of servers all around the world. It is used to provide rich media such as images, videos, and audio with high-speed delivery. Magento is built in order to support CDN functionality without any third-party applications. It is necessary to have a CDN setup if your extension will process heavy media, such as high resolution product pictures or videos.

Redis and Memcached

Redis and Memcached are two popular solutions for performance optimization. These two cache engines have a lot of similarities in the way they work. They store cached content in the RAM of your server in order to deliver it faster. Both of them are in-memory, key-value data stores and they use the NoSQL data management solution.

Because it's stored in the cache memory, the size of the data is limited. Your server will reply to a request without making an additional request to the database if the asked-for value is in the cache.

Redis is newer and often preferred over the "old" Memcached. It has more functionalities than Memcached, but it has a lower speed performance.

> Magento suggests using Memcached for session storage, even if Redis also handles this feature.
>
> Find out all the information about Redis and Memcached on the Magento 2 documentation website: http://devdocs.magento.com/guides/v2.0/config-guide/redis/config-redis.html.

How to measure your speed optimization

There are some useful tools available to work with your Magento installation, which enforce your monitoring, measuring, and speed optimization.

New Relic

New Relic is a powerful analysis software platform. It provides a wide range of real-time data to measure the performance of your server. The setup consists of deploying a PHP extension to collect data from your application and a local proxy daemon to send it to New Relic.

Overviewing the dashboard

The dashboard of New Relic looks like the following screenshot:

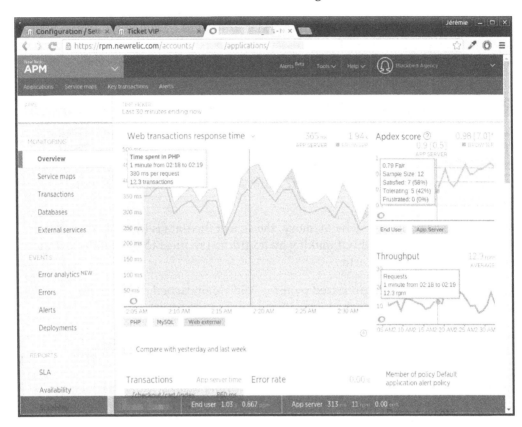

An overview of New Relic's services will give you an insight into what is happening in your website. It will provide you with data on the transaction time (type of transaction, source, and so on). You can track the real-time **Apdex score** (top right). This rate is the global user satisfaction, based on a set threshold. The application's owner defines a response time threshold (for example, 2.00 seconds) and all the responses handled below this limit will be considered as a satisfied user. The **Apdex score** is a ratio value of the number of satisfied requests to the number of total requests made. The goal is to have an Apdex score of 1, which means all users are satisfied.

Tracking transactions

The **Transactions** page is a summary of the tiniest transaction details. This data will help you track the page with the slowest response time, the most dissatisfying Apdex score, or the highest throughput. All these measurements are key indicators to find the source of the optimization problem. Here's an overview of the **Transactions** page:

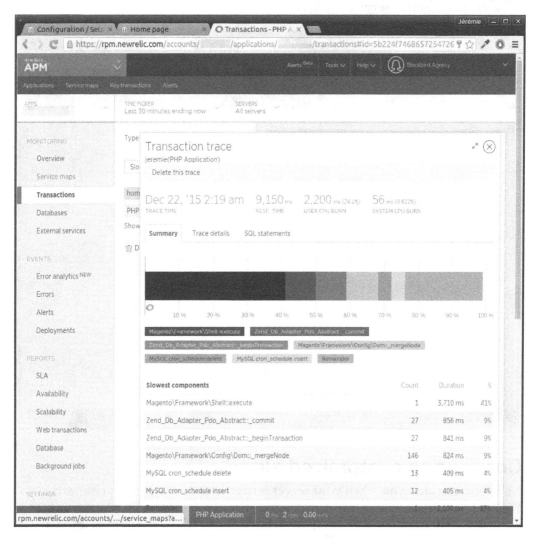

The **Transaction trace** tab will give you hints on where your overloading comes from. It's a very helpful feature to define which pages of your website have potential performance issues.

External services monitoring

Using external services is often tricky. Even if you lose control to a third-party application, New Relic will provide you feedback on the performance of these APIs. Like the HTTP transaction with your server, you can also track the time consumption, the average response time, or the throughput **RPM** (**requests per minute**) of an external service:

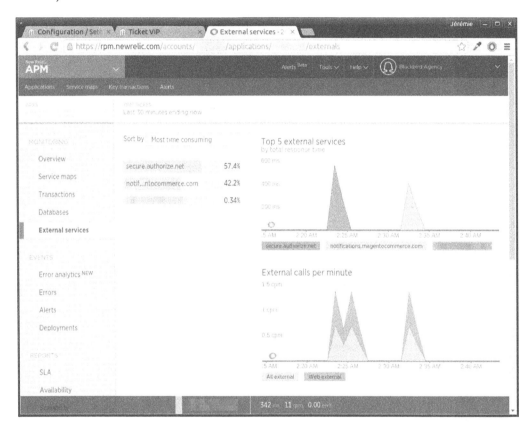

Configuring customized alerts

New Relic can alert you when your server is overloaded with custom notifications. You will be notified when your Apdex score is under the threshold you have configured. For example, if your Apdex score is under 0.7 (which means less than 70% of the requests are "satisfied"), you will get an alert by e-mail or on your mobile phone explaining the current issue.

The first step is to create alert policies (custom alerts):

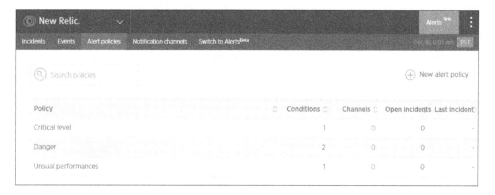

The second step is to set custom conditions that will trigger the alerts. For example, you can configure a **Critical level** alert if the Apdex score of your server is under 0.5 for 10 minutes:

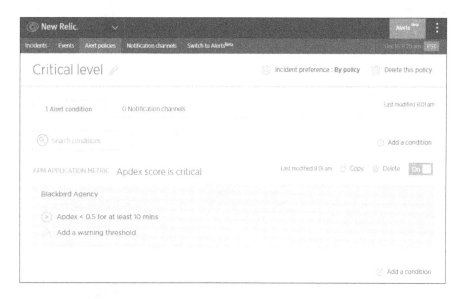

New Relic allows you to set several conditions for a unique alert policy. This feature will help you organize the different conditions for your alerts. The last step of your alert setup is to choose how you want to be notified.

 In **Events | Alerts**, you can follow the history of your alerts and have an overview of all the latest reports you received, for example, how long they lasted and what the source of the problem was.

Service Level Agreement reports

Service Level Agreement (**SLA**) reports will allow you monitor day-by-day metrics on your websites. Your SLA reports are available via **Reports | SLA**.

New Relic is useful for tracking user satisfaction through the load time and the Apdex score. These measures are relevant because they give you insights into what the user experience was at any given moment. The SLA reports provide such data to you on a daily basis. Tracking the variations in your loading time or Apdex score is essential in order to monitor your optimization process:

Browser

So far, we tracked the performance on the server side. New Relic also measures the client side to track potential weaknesses. This data is available in the **BROWSER** menu. For example, you can track throughput on different browsers:

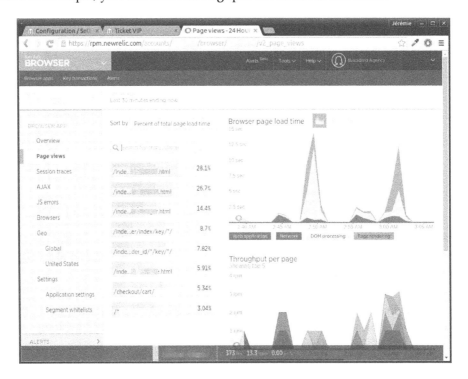

Some other browser-oriented features are relevant in a performance optimization strategy. The JS error-tracking feature will give you data about JS errors in the user's browser. As a developer, the transmitted error code will help you reproduce and correct this bug.

Configure your Magento backend to enhance your experience with New Relic.

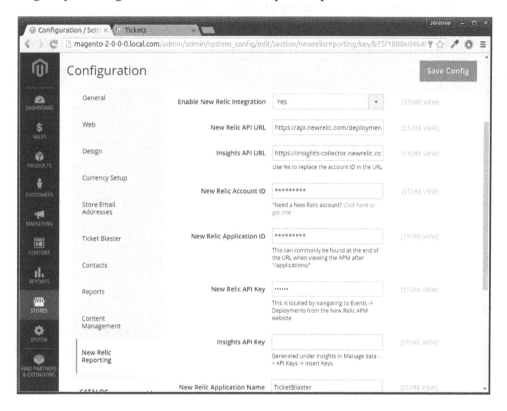

Quanta monitoring

Several solutions can provide metrics for server loads, as New Relic does. Quanta is a performance optimizer dedicated to Magento stores. It provides real-time data on the default pages of your store, such as the **Account**, **Category**, or **Product** pages. There are not as many features as New Relic, but the live covering feature is easier and more user-friendly. The merchant-oriented interface of Quanta provides a global approach to the real-time performance of a Magento store:

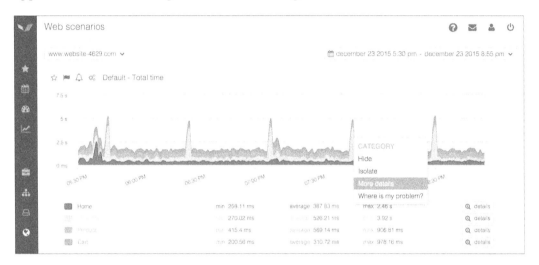

Web scenarios

A web scenario is a series of visited pages (steps) executed one after another. It closely resembles the behavior of a real visitor to your website. When a step has an error, the web scenario stops and does not perform the following steps. Red bars will appear on the graphs.

Web scenarios are the main feature of Quanta computing and are really helpful to ensure that, in addition to the eventual errors a page can generate, the page itself renders the expected content.

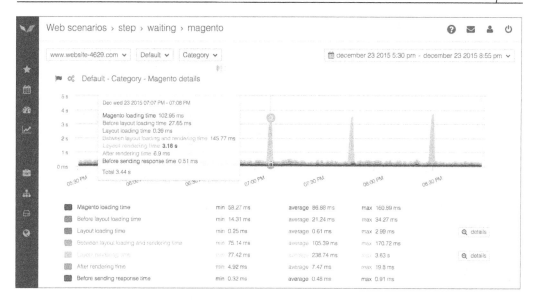

Application profiling

The Magento profiling module allows us to analyze all the application's layers and helps the developer to optimize the block with one click.

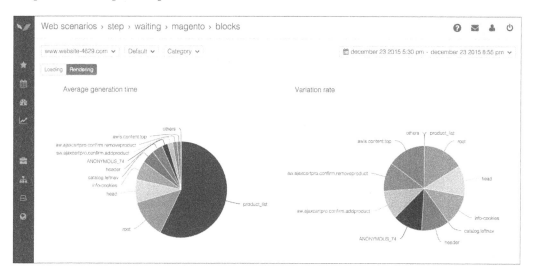

Google Analytics

Google Analytics is a complete solution to watch all the behaviors of your store. Analyzing this data will help you to track the results of your optimization strategy.

 You can set up a Google Analytics account for your store via **Store | Configuration | Sales | Google API**.

Google Analytics will provide you with information on the bounce rate or average time spent in your store. Your optimization strategy can be tracked with these two indicators. Always keep in mind that these two indicators cannot be positive with a slow website.

YSlow

YSlow analyzes web pages in order to define why they're running slow. It's based on 34 Yahoo! standards, such as the number of HTTP requests, the `gzip` components, the use of a CDN, minify JS and CSS, the ETags configuration, making favicons small and cacheable, and so on.

This tool is available as a browser extension (for Google Chrome, Mozilla Firefox, Safari, and Opera) but can also be set up with the source code, which is downloadable from `https://github.com/marcelduran/yslow`.

YSlow will give you different data on key aspects of your speed optimization. For example, it will give you an overview of the HTTP requests made to your server.

Look at the following two images. The first is the result of YSlow before JS/CSS minify, while the second is after JS/CSS minify.

Before JS/CSS minify, the result is as follows:

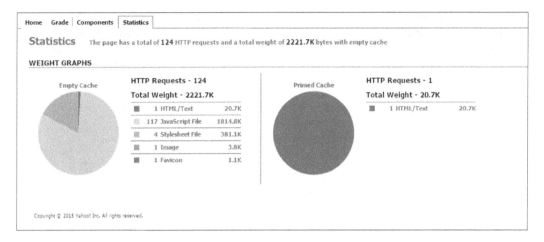

After JS/CSS minify, the result is as follows:

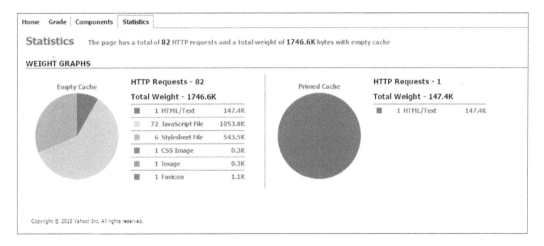

This data will provide an overview on your speed optimization process and track the performance of the different tools you used to reduce the load of your server.

GTMetrix

GTMetrix is a powerful performance tracking tool. It provides summarized key performance indicators such as the load time, page size, and number of requests. GTMetrix will give you tips on how to improve the performance. These recommendations concern parameters such as CSS/JS minifying, `gzip` compression, asynchronous processes, and image optimization.

GTMetrix provides free access to a lot of these features. The professional version has additional functionalities such as monitoring from remote locations, alert triggering, or scheduling successive analysis.

Summary

In this chapter, we covered all the main powerful tools that can drive the performance research you have to perform during extension development. Thanks to these analyses, you can be sure to provide to your customers with the best code for their projects.

In the next chapter, we'll discuss etiquette and the best practice to prevent our module from being a source of woe for our customers.

7
Module Creation Etiquette

In this chapter, we will discuss the etiquette behind creating third-party extensions. Yes, our extension is now optimized for speed and it is fully bug-free, as we have seen in the previous chapter. Nevertheless, our customers trust us by purchasing our module and installing the software on their systems. We must prevent our extension from being a source of woe for our customers.

Some of the following parts will not seem immediately necessary to you because you are a "simple" extension editor. Keep in mind that these are important concepts that are found in all development projects and this culture will be in your extensions code.

For sure, a completely secure system is impossible, so the best approach you can use is to gauge the risk and usability, and ensure that your code does not degrade the security level of your customers' Magento infrastructure.

Do not underestimate the risk; the Internet is filled with people trying to break your code and crash your client's website just for fun or for ransom. At the beginning of my career, a client said to me, "I'm a little seller. No one is interested in me. Please don't charge me at all for features that concern the security, and don't develop any control." Two months later, the website was hacked and the homepage was modified with a political message and the hacker's signature. Since then, all my developments take into account what is going to follow.

In this chapter, we will look at:

- The possible attacks on your extension
- The Payment Card Industry Data Security Standard
- Software considerations

The possible attacks

In order to know how to prevent and fix vulnerabilities, we have to know the possible attacks your extension can undergo.

SQL injection

This is the most common attack and maybe the easiest to perform against a website that is not protected. The malicious user enters SQL statements in form fields in order to modify the way your script works.

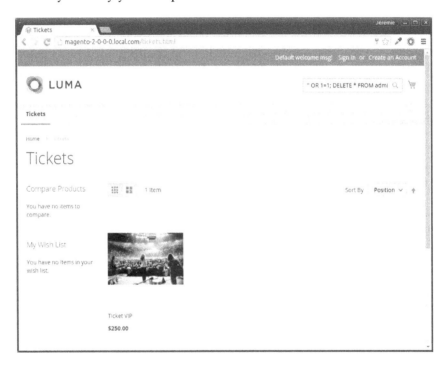

Magento worked hard on this point, and it is fully equipped to permit you to secure all your forms and databases requests.

Here is an example of the `Magento\Customer\Model\ResourceModel\Customer::_beforeSave()` method. We can see that the `email` parameter isn't written directly in the request, but it is declared as something like a variable:

```
$bind = ['email' => $customer->getEmail()];
$select = $connection->select()->from(
        $this->getEntityTable(),
        [$this->getEntityIdField()]
    )->where(
```

```
                 'email = :email'
            );
    $result = $connection->fetchOne($select, $bind);
```

This is a prepared request. If we open the declaration of the where clause, we will have to open `Magento\Framework\DB\Select::where()` that is an overload of `Zend_Db_Select::where()`. This method calls the `_where()` method of the same class.

Now it gets interesting; the request is formatted by `Zend_Db_Adapter_Abstract::quoteInto()` that uses the `quote()` method. This is the most important method in our case, because it sanitizes and returns an SQL-safe value for our request.

> For more information, visit the following URLs:
>
> `http://php.net/manual/en/pdo.prepared-statements.php`
> `http://framework.zend.com/manual/1.12/en/zend.db.adapter.html`

Cross-site scripting

Cross-site scripting (XSS) is, like SQL injection, one of the most common attacks. The attacker uses vulnerabilities on the website to inject client-side script into the web pages viewed by other users. The main goal is to steal personal information or authentication sessions.

There are two types of XSS: the non-persistent and the persistent XSS.

Non-persistent

This is by far the most common type of XSS.

As a simple example, your website proposes a search engine that displays on the result page the searched string. Try it!

```
<form action="index.php" method="POST">

<p>Search: </p>
<input type="text" size="40" name="search" />
<input type="submit" value="Submit"/>

</form>

<?php
```

```
if(isset($_POST['search'])){
   echo "Your request was:".$_POST['search'];
}
```

Now enter in the text field the following string and click on **Submit**:

```
<script>alert("you've been hacked!")</script>
```

We get the following result:

Note that my screenshot does not provide data from the Google Chrome browser, which detected (with the same code) the potential XSS attack. The browser doesn't fire `alert()` and highlights the code source, as shown in the following screenshot:

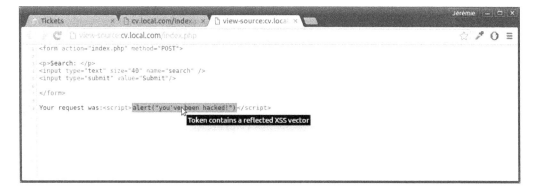

Persistent

The persistent XSS vulnerability is a more devastating variant of a XSS flaw because the data is saved by the server and permanently displayed to other users. The method is the same as the non-persistent attack: a script is displayed on the page in order to try to get authorization cookies or secret information.

In order to protect your code, use as many possible `Zend_Validate` methods as described in *Chapter 3, Best Practices and Scaling for the Web*. The most common is the pattern validation.

Here is an example from the `ForgotPasswordPost` class of the `Magento\Customer\Controller\Account` namespace:

```
if (!\Zend_Validate::is($email, 'EmailAddress')) {
    $this->_getSession()->setForgottenEmail($email);
    $this->messageManager->addError(__('Please correct the email
address.'));
    $resultRedirect->setPath('*/*/forgotpassword');
return $returnRedirect;
}
```

In your templates, use the following codes:

```
<?php echo $block->escapeHtml($block->getTitle()) ?>
<?php echo $block->escapeXssInUrl($block->getUrl()) ?>
```

 See how Magento takes measures against XSS attacks here: http://
devdocs.magento.com/guides/v2.0/frontend-dev-guide/
templates/template-security.html.

Cross-site request forgeries

Unlike XSS, which exploits the trust a user has for a particular website, **cross-site request forgeries (CSRF)** exploits the trust that a website has in a user's browser.

If an attacker is able to find a reproducible link that executes a specific action on the target page while the victim is being logged in, he is able to embed such a link on a page he controls and trick the victim into opening it.

In Magento, every form has been protected against CSRF attacks since the 1.7.x version. Look at the source code of a simple form, such as the customer login:

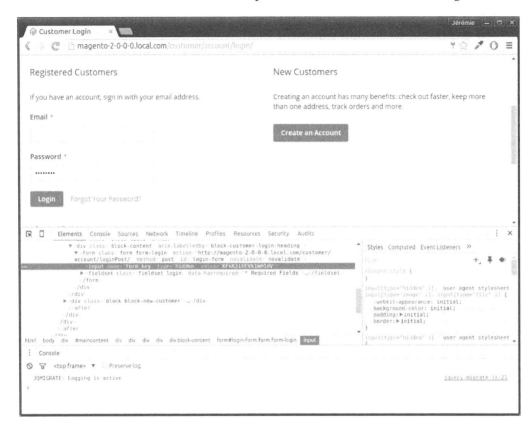

This code is simply generated by the following little snippet:

```php
<?php echo $this->getBlockHtml('formkey'); ?>
```

It can be validated by the following:

```php
$this->formKeyValidator->validate($this->getRequest())
```

 Read `Magento\Customer\Controller\Account\LoginPost::execute()` for a good example of how Magento works with it.

The Payment Card Industry Data Security Standard

The **Payment Card Industry Data Security Standard (PCI DSS)** is a set of requirements designed to ensure that all companies that process, store, or transmit credit card information maintain a secure environment.

It specifies 12 requirements for compliance organized into six logically related groups called "control objectives". They are as follows:

- Build and maintain a secure network:
    - Install and maintain a firewall configuration to protect cardholder data
    - Do not use vendor-supplied defaults for system passwords and other security parameters

- Protect cardholder data:
    - Protect stored cardholder data
    - Encrypt transmission of cardholder data across open, public networks

- Maintain a vulnerability management program:
    - Use and regularly update antivirus software on all systems commonly affected by malware
    - Develop and maintain secure systems and applications

- Implement strong access control measures:
    - Restrict access to cardholder data by business need-to-know
    - Assign a unique ID to each person with computer access
    - Restrict physical access to cardholder data.

- Regularly monitor and test networks:
    - Track and monitor all access to network resources and cardholder data
    - Regularly test security systems and processes

- Maintain an information security policy:
    - Maintain a policy that addresses information security

Usually, as an extension editor, you don't have to be PCI-compliant yourself. But your customers (merchants) sometimes have to be. Your role is at least to be able to advise them.

In case you propose a payment extension that's different, you have to be able to deliver through your code a PCI-compliant architecture that permits your customer to be a part of it. That's what we will see in the following parts by developing points 3 and 4 of the PCI DSS.

Protecting stored cardholder data

The best practice when protecting cardholder data is not to store it. It seems logical, but it is the best solution for ensuring that the data is as secure as possible.

Many payment solutions work without any data storage on your server, such as PayPal. If you choose this option, you won't have to be PCI-compliant yourself because you are not storing credit card information on your server. In this case, you have to consider that your customers will be redirected to the website of the payment processor and will have to leave your website, which might be inconvenient and interrupt the buying process.

If ever you have to store cardholder data, you have to look at the `sales_order_payment` table structure and read the following classes: `Magento\EncryptionKey\Model\ResourceModel\Key\Change` and especially its method `_reEncryptCreditCardNumbers()`.

The `$this->encryptor->encrypt()` call is made on a `Magento\Framework\Encryption\ Encryptor` model object.

Finally, `getCrypt()` returns a new `Magento\Framework\Encryption\Crypt` object.

Encrypt transmissions

Always use SSL to transmit any personal information.

This is obviously true for any sensitive data, such as cardholder information or personal details of your customers. But transmissions that are more than one year should be encrypted. This first ensures that your website's users have better private protection against network listeners or spies. And now HTTPS is a ranking factor too!

[Read more about the PCI DSS and its administration here: `http://www.pcisecuritystandards.org`.]

Developing your own payment method

Magento 2 completely remastered the checkout steps and based the date exchange on a REST API. Server-side web APIs are built with a new M2 Service Contracts approach. One of the benefits of this new method is that checkout form is now designed to be compact enough to easily fill in all the data using a mobile or tablet.

We will see here how to propose to your customer a new custom offline payment method, which can be coupled to your extension. We will call it money.

Implementing the method

The method will be rendered as an UI component, in a dedicated `javascript` file:

1. Create the file `[extension_path]/view/frontend/web/js/view/payment/method-renderer/ticketblaster-money.js` and add the following code:

```
define(
    [
        'Magento_Checkout/js/view/payment/default'
    ],
    function (Component) {
        'use strict';
        return Component.extend({
            defaults: {
                template: 'Blackbird_TicketBlaster/payment/
ticketblaster-money'
            },
        });
    }
);
```

2. Create the file `[extension_path]/view/frontend/web/js/view/payment/ticketblaster.js` and add the following code:

```
/*browser:true*/
/*global define*/
define(
    [
        'uiComponent',
        'Magento_Checkout/js/model/payment/renderer-list'
    ],
    function (
        Component,
        rendererList
    ) {
```

```
        'use strict';
        rendererList.push(
            {
                type: 'monetico_onetime',
                component: 'Blackbird_TicketBlaster/js/view/
payment/method-renderer/ticketblaster-money'
            }
        );
        /** Add view logic here if needed */
        return Component.extend({});
    }
);
```

This file will register the renderer we just created with the parameter component.

1. Create the file [extension_path]/view/frontend/web/template/
   payment/ticketblaster-money.html and add the following code:

```
<div class="payment-method" data-bind="css: {'_active': (getCode()
== isChecked())}">
    <div class="payment-method-title field choice">
        <input type="radio"
                name="payment[method]"
                class="radio"
                data-bind="attr: {'id': getCode()}, value:
getCode(), checked: isChecked, click: selectPaymentMethod,
visible: isRadioButtonVisible()"/>
        <label class="label"><span>Money method</span></label>
    </div>

    <div class="payment-method-content">
        <div class="payment-method-billing-address">
            <!-- ko foreach: $parent.getRegion(getBillingAddressFo
rmName()) -->
            <!-- ko template: getTemplate() --><!-- /ko -->
            <!--/ko-->
        </div>
        <div class="actions-toolbar">
            <div class="primary">
                <button class="action primary checkout"
                        type="submit"
                        data-bind="
                        click: placeOrder,
                        attr: {title: $t('Place Order')},
                        enable: (getCode() == isChecked()),
```

```
                        css: {disabled:
    !isPlaceOrderActionAllowed()}
                            "
                        disabled>
                  <span data-bind="i18n: 'Place Order'"></span>
              </button>
          </div>
        </div>
      </div>
    </div>
```

2. Create the file [extension_path]/view/frontend/layout/checkout_
   index_index.xml and add the following code:

```xml
<?xml version="1.0"?>
<page xmlns:xsi="http://www.w3.org/2001/XMLSchema-instance"
layout="1column" xsi:noNamespaceSchemaLocation="urn:magento:framew
ork:View/Layout/etc/page_configuration.xsd">
<body>
    <referenceBlock name="checkout.root">
        <arguments>
            <argument name="jsLayout" xsi:type="array">
                <item name="components" xsi:type="array">
                    <item name="checkout" xsi:type="array">
                        <item name="children" xsi:type="array">
                            <item name="steps" xsi:type="array">
                                <item name="children"
xsi:type="array">
                                    <item name="billing-step"
xsi:type="array">
                                        <item name="component"
xsi:type="string">uiComponent</item>
                                        <item name="children"
xsi:type="array">
                                            <item name="payment"
xsi:type="array">
                                                <item
name="children" xsi:type="array">
                                                    <item
name="renders" xsi:type="array">
                                                        <item
name="children" xsi:type="array">

<item name="ticketblaster" xsi:type="array">

<item name="component" xsi:type="string">Blackbird_TicketBlaster/
js/view/payment/ticketblaster</item>
```

```
<item name="methods" xsi:type="array">

<item name="ticketblaster_money" xsi:type="array">

<item name="isBillingAddressRequired" xsi:type="boolean">true</
item>

</item>

</item>

                                                                  </
item>

                                                            </
item>

                                              </item>
                                        </item>
                                    </item>
                                </item>
                            </item>
                        </item>
                    </item>
                </item>
            </item>
        </item>
      </argument>
    </arguments>
   </referenceBlock>
 </body>
 </page>
```

This layout file will declare the payment method in the checkout layout by overloading it.

1. Go to the checkout page by adding a product to your cart to ensure that the method is activated.

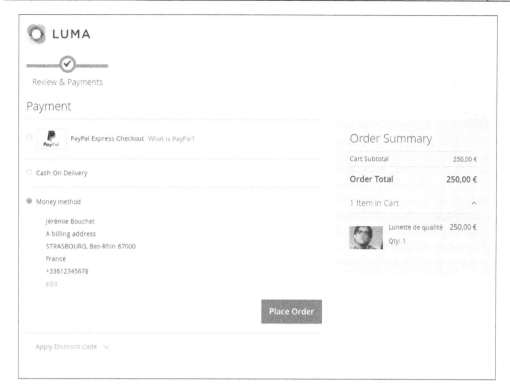

 Read the API documentation of Magento at `http://devdocs.magento.com/swagger/index.html` and read the other default payment methods to learn how they work (especially `vendors/magento/module-offline-payments`).

Software considerations

Keep in mind that a lot of your clients don't upgrade their system (for many reasons). I'm not telling you to not be always up to date with software versions, but learn to switch between different development environments that run different versions of PHP, Apache, Memcached, and so on.

PHP

Magento 2 has natively supported PHP 7 since the first release. We all agree that PHP 7 performs better; it is faster and contains a lot of new functionalities. In this case, it is logical to run the Magento extension project on PHP 7. Nevertheless, you may have some other projects that don't need this new version, or worse: they can't work with it.

We will see how to compile and run PHP 7 for the specific vhost of your server. I will assume that your server is Debian-based, that you are the root user, and you use nginx, which has already been installed and configured.

Installing PHP

Here's how you go about it:

2. First, install some useful packages, which we will need later:

   ```
   apt-get install vim bzip2 build-essential libxml2-dev
   ```

3. Download the PHP 7 sources:

   ```
   cd /usr/local/src
   wget http://us2.php.net/distributions/php-7.0.2.tar.bz2
   tar xjf php-7.0.2.tar.bz2
   cd php-7.0.2
   ```

    Read this page to see the latest available version: http://us2.php.net/downloads.php.

4. Create the folder that will contain PHP:

   ```
   mkdir -p /usr/local/php7
   ```

5. Execute the following command to prepare the compilation of PHP:

   ```
   export OPTIM=-02
   ./configure --prefix=/usr/local/php7 \
           --enable-fpm
           --with-xsl \
           --enable-soap \
           --with-gettext \
           --enable-mbstring --with-mbstring=all \
           --disable-debug \
   ```

```
            --enable-memory-limit \
            --enable-ftp \
            --with-mcrypt \
            --enable-zip \
            --enable-calendar \
            --enable-exif \
            --enable-pdo \
            --with-pdo-mysql \
            --with-mysql \
            --with-pdo-sqlite \
            --with-sqlite \
            --with-zlib \
            --with-jpeg-dir \
            --with-gd \
            --with-freetype-dir=DIR \
            --with-imap-ssl \
            --with-kerberos \
            --with-imap \
            --with-curl \
            --enable-bcmath \
    make
    make install
```

Configuring PHP

Because we didn't install PHP 7 with the `distrib` packages, we have to configure it by ourselves. Here's how you do it:

1. Configure PHP with the default `config` file by running the following commands (you can configure it later according to your specific needs):

    ```
    cd /usr/local/php7/etc/
    cp php-fpm.conf.default php-fpm.conf
    ```

2. Edit the file `/usr/local/php7/etc/php-fpm.conf` and uncomment the following line:

    ```
    pid = run/php7-fpm.pid
    ```

3. Create the default pool of `php-fpm`:

    ```
    cd php-fpm.d
    cp www.conf.default www.conf
    ```

4. Edit the `www.conf` file and update the lines according to the following values:

```
user = www-data
group = www-data
listen = /var/run/php7-fpm.sock
listen.owner = www-data
listen.group = www-data
listen.mode = 0660
```

5. Prepare the `php.ini` file by getting the default one provided in the sources:

```
cp /usr/local/src/php-7.0.2/php.ini-production /usr/local/php7/
lib/php.ini
```

6. Make `php-fpm` launchable at server startup:

```
cp /usr/local/src/php-7.0.2/sapi/fpm/init.d.php-fpm.in /etc/
init.d/php7-fpm

chmod 755 /etc/init.d/php7-fpm

insserv php7-fpm

cp /usr/local/src/php-7.0.2/sapi/fpm/php-fpm.service.in /lib/
systemd/system/php7-fpm.service

systemctl enable php7-fpm.service

systemctl daemon-reload

systemctl enable php7-fpm
```

7. We can now launch `php7-fpm`:

```
service php7-fpm start
```

Configuring nginx

The following are the steps to configure nginx:

1. Open your `vhost` configuration file (the one you use for your `TicketBlaster` extension, for example) and update the location instruction by adding the following lines:

```
location ~ \.php$ {
            include snippets/fastcgi-php.conf;
    #
    #       # With php5-cgi alone:
    #       fastcgi_pass 127.0.0.1:9000;
    #       # With php5-fpm:
            fastcgi_pass unix:/var/run/php7-fpm.sock;
}
```

There are three projects that are written to do the same thing:

- `https://github.com/c9s/phpbrew`
- `https://github.com/CHH/phpenv`
- `https://github.com/wilmoore/php-version`

PSR-1 to PSR-7

The PHP Standards Recommendations will help you to keep a high-level of coding, which protects you against a lot of security issues.

Read them here: `http://www.php-fig.org/psr/`.

OWASP

The **Open Web Application Security Project (OWASP)** edits a developer guide and a testing guide is freely available here: `https://www.owasp.org`.

Stay tuned

Magento and the community communicate a lot about security issues. Follow them and read carefully the posts they publish.

Follow, sign up, and read:

- `https://magento.com/security`
- `https://github.com/magento/magento2/issues`

Summary

In this chapter, we dealt with an important quantity of notions of security, which act as the mainstay of the best practices of development. You obviously have to read carefully the sources I shared here and always work cautiously while you develop any extension which is to be shared with the community. Your reputation and the security of your clients are at stake.

In the next chapter, we will discuss how to protect your intellectual property while sharing your code to the community.

8
Optimization for Teamwork Development

Teamwork development is a matter of good practice and common sense. Some managers make the mistake of considering developers as a pure resource—a coding robot. It is essential to shape your working process to your team. However, there are some key methods that you cannot skip in your development process and a version control system is one of them.

As we saw in *Chapter 1*, *Introduction to Extension Development*, Git is one of the most widely used code management systems.

Git is based on a system of branches; it's a nonlinear development system where each branch is a different state of your code. Thus, the ways of managing branches are numerous and can refer to different models. That's what we will see in this chapter.

Briefly, we'll be looking at:

- Version control and code management
- Feature branch workflow
- Project management methodology
- Communication with a developer team

Version control and code management

The "best" workflow does not exist and it's why you need to create, develop, and improve yours. Of course, some guidelines exist and they will provide you with a framework of good practices. These standardized models are very similar, so you just need to take advantage of each model and build your own Git workflow.

Usually, we call the main branch *master*, which represents the trunk of your developments.

Feature branch workflow

This section is an introduction to the specific workflow called "feature branch". It's based on the following branches:

- Master
- Develop
- Feature
- Release
- Hotfix

Master branch

This is the first branch your repository will contain and it is the default one. Usually, the branch designates the main trunk of the developments on which the others are based.

Another way of using the **Master** branch is to reflect the production: a version which is committed on the master exists in the production environment.

Develop branch

We create a **Develop** branch, reflecting the latest updates from your development team.

All the multiple developments will be added to the **Develop** branch instead of being added directly to the master. However, in our model, developers will not commit their code directly on develop either!

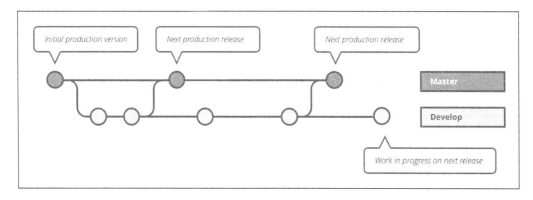

Imagine you are a developer (for example, your name is DevB) who wants to create a new feature. Your colleague, DevA, has already began to develop another new feature and commit the first pieces of code on the **Develop** branch (firstly, to save his job). The code written by DevA isn't already fully functional and causes some bugs. Because of that, you are unable to begin writing your own new feature! That's why we use specific branches for each feature.

Feature branches

The developer creates a **Feature** branch for each different functionality.

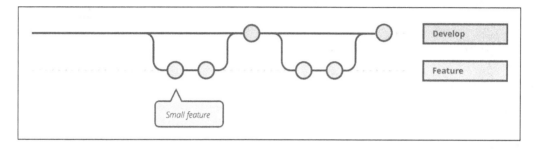

If two developers are working at the same time on different features, each of the teammates will create a different branch feature for their own feature without impacting the **Develop** branch. Once the developer has finished his feature, they will merge it to develop. The typical aspect of a **Feature** branch is that it exists as long as the feature is in development. Small features developed by only one developer will not necessarily be relevant to the other collaborators, so they will not import these remote branches to their local environment.

The small feature will be committed on the **Feature** branch and then merged to develop; the other developers are not involved in this process.

If the development concerns a big feature involving different developers and with a high level of complexity and workload, every member has to checkout this feature branch and commit and push their code on it.

The **Feature** branches must never interact with the **Master** branch. When a feature is done, it's merged to its parent branch, **Develop**. Afterwards, the development will be merged to **Master** and get deployed.

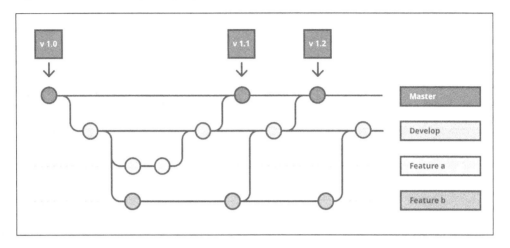

Release branches

Even if you keep the **Master** branch as an almost perfect replica of your online store, you can still get a bad surprise when you deploy your latest features. Placing the **Release** branch between your **Develop** and **Master** branches will allow you to have a compatibility bridge. Always keep in mind that your **Develop** branch is the desired state you want to have in the **Master** branch. So, if you have any current issues or you are not ready for deployment developments in the **Develop** branch, you may have conflicts and bugs after merging them in the **Master** branch.

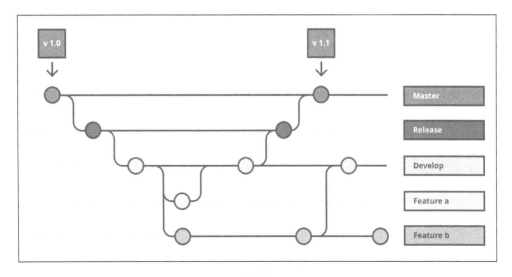

The main purpose of your **Release** branch is to be the "buffer area" between your further **Release** branch and your production environment. For instance, if you develop a feature A and wait for a feature B before releasing version 2.0 of your website, you will put feature A in a quasi-production environment (the **Release** branch must be an almost perfect replication of the **Master** branch); perform the tests, and wait in this buffer area before deploying your version 2.0. Using this **Release** branch will provide more freedom to your **Develop** branch. Indeed, any small change on the **Develop** branch can affect feature A or B. By merging this feature to the **Release** branch, you guarantee a level of stability to your development process and can avoid conflicts or overriding.

Hotfix branch

Hotfix branches are used to quickly correct a bug in the production environment. While you are deploying a new release on production, your developer team will continue to work on your **Develop** branch. In case of a critical bug, you will be in conflict if you correct it on **Develop** and merge it immediately to **Master**. Some of the collaborators' development can be committed and pushed to **Develop**, but not necessarily achieved. By fixing the bug on the **Develop** branch, you will merge the undergoing developments on the **Master** branch.

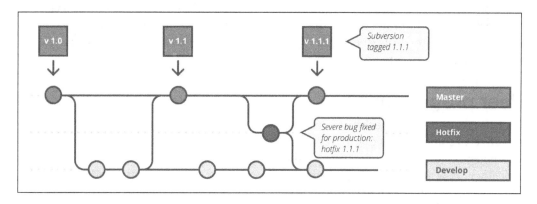

As soon as the bug is fixed, it should be merged to the **Master** and **Develop** branches. Having a dedicated branch for hotfixes will avoid a workflow interruption in case there is a major bug on production.

The workflow presented is just one of the many ways you can build your development process. Always remember that you need to adapt these methodologies to your environment, and not the opposition branches. If you are in a small team and you think correcting bugs on the **Develop** branch can be handled, don't go for a **Hotfix** branch. It's all a matter of getting inspired by a framework to build your own model.

Deployment and backups

It can be relevant to automate your deployment process. Without autodeployment, you need to transfer the modified code to your server by FTP or SFTP. Wouldn't it be easier and faster to automate this process?

Webhooks are used to pull an event after they are triggered by another one. In our example, we can trigger the deployment after the Git push of the master branch. When a development is finished, tested, and merged to the master, it will then automatically be deployed on your production environment. Git will check the hooks directory to see whether there is a script associated with the Git command push.

Backup strategy

Backup strategy is also a model you need to think about. Some companies prefer to have a daily automatic backup model for databases and source code. Using a simple `Git clone` command in a daily-triggered script will provide you added safety. Also, try not to set up your backup on the same server.

Compressing your backup

Your backup strategy must consider the storage limitation of your backup server. The cost issue is shaping most of the choices in backup strategies. It's why you need to use compression tools in order to reduce your directory size. Lots of tools provide a high compression rate without data loss.

Peer programming

Peer programming is a technique where two developers code together on the same screen. It is considered a controversial method by code purists. For a long time, it was considered as a time-wasting method, whereas now it is accepted as improving efficiency. Peer programming is not simply watching your colleague coding. Usually, the developer with more experience is observing and reviewing his collaborator while he is coding. In this way, the less experienced one does not get bored by watching a code master develop at the speed of light. Both are active during peer programming sessions with a high productivity rate.

Developing standards and code review

The standards must not make you lose more time than it will help you save. You can set up different level of standards (mandatory, important, or recommended) and define the content and the hierarchy of these standards with your team. Too many rules will give an unpleasant feeling to the developers and may cause a drop in productivity. It's all a matter of finding the balance. You can, for example, set the indentation rules as mandatory. It's a good way to have similarities among different developers without affecting the productivity.

Reviewing the code of a junior developer is a clever way to speed up his learning process. It's not a matter of correcting his mistakes, but is essentially a dialog on the choices made by the junior developer and a discussion on the areas of improvement.

Of course, peer programming and code reviewing will create a productivity reduction in the short term. You need to consider this as a required step for growing your production capacity in the long term. Nowadays, diffusing knowledge inside the team is a key factor of successful companies.

Project management methodology

Many of the web agencies claim to work with the agile methodology. We will not look deeply into this project management philosophy because many different books or articles have already covered this topic. I will give you a few headlines on how to optimize your working process with different case studies.

Why are the agile methods more adapted for extension development on Magento? The answer is obvious if we consider that the only alternate solution is the Waterfall model. Many researchers have shown the limits of the antique Waterfall model through statistical reviews. Indeed, in modern project management history, the Waterfall method highlights a high failure rate (for more information, refer to *Scaling Software Agility, Dean Leffingwell, 2007*). Basically, the Waterfall model has disastrous consequences in the case of scope changing (and it's highly likely that it will happen in your projects). The entire project will be affected if only one task is blocking your team.

This is why the iterative approach of agile methodology is essential to your project management. It is crucial to have flexible/parallel phases (for example: requirements, design, integration, development, test, and deployment). But never forget that you are using the tool, not the opposition. Don't use an irrelevant process just because it's part of a specific methodology.

Communicating in a developer team

Your project management workflow must be a continuous reflection. To build the most efficient way to work, you have to learn from your previous experiences and adjust your process for your team. Obviously, communication has a key role in the performance of your development team, but it is not enough. This process must be a basic good practice of your team, not an added value to your development method. Never underestimate the impact of a small talk with your coworker; you have more to learn by listening to a colleague's advice than by thinking on your own. People always see asking for help as a weakness, while in reality it is a proper way to improve productivity and progress as a team.

Communication optimization can rely on several tools. The goal of this chapter is not to show an exhaustive list of methods for improving the communication in your team. However, it will give you a few tips.

An instant messaging tool is essential for your team. Even if some of your colleagues use it to share funny cat GIFs, it has a prominent place in your teamwork optimization strategy.

Team awareness of workflow

It's important to get your teammates involved in your philosophy; your corporate DNA. This spirit is built with high employee engagement in their projects, meetings, clear and small objectives, rewards after meeting goals, post-delivery feedbacks from everyone involved, and so on. The list is not exhaustive; the techniques are various, but the goal is the same: increasing relevant communication and making them feel helpful.

The inevitable tool of a team of developers is the well-known agile whiteboard. It will provide a global overview of your current workflow, undergoing projects, and regarding your project management model, an insight of your colleagues' progress.

Slack

Slack is a cloud-based collaboration tool that you can synchronize with plenty of third-party services. It is the main competitor of Hipchat, the solution proposed by Atlassian.

With Slack, you will get a centralized communication system for all your tools, including:

- Repository services, such as GitHub
- Project management tools, such as Jira, Trello, and more

- Customer relations tools, such as Zendesk
- File hosting systems, such as Google Drive or DropBox
- Performance monitoring software, such as New Relic
- Social media accounts, such as Facebook, LinkedIn, and Twitter
- Google services, such as Agenda, Gmail, Drive, and more

The following screenshot shows the **#releases** screen:

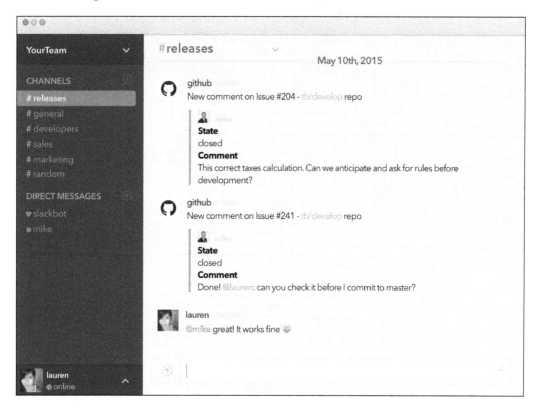

The synchronization between all your production tools and an internal communication tool will increase the awareness and input of your team members. You can customize Slack to get good information to the good collaborator without useless noise. Slack is just a tool; your internal communication strategy will shape its impact.

Summary

In this chapter, we addressed all the main tools to optimize your teamwork development by discovering version control or new project management methods.

In the next chapter, we will see how to publish TicketBlaster and other extensions you created for the Magento Marketplace and how to sell it by yourself.

9
Magento Marketplace

Our module is now built. We now have the task of submitting the module to the Magento Marketplace, the Magento website for distributing free and paid extensions. We will see how publishing a free and a paid extension on the Magento Marketplace works and how Magento controls it to limit plagiarism.

In this chapter, we'll dive into:

- Magento Marketplace
- The Magento Extension Distribution & Service Agreement
- Selling extensions by ourselves

 As of the writing of this chapter, Magento Marketplace is not yet online, so some of the information provided here may differ in the future.

The new Connect is called Marketplace

You probably already know that Magento 2 is a major new version of the e-commerce solution and that the extensions for the 1.x version were distributed over the Magento Connect platform. With the growth of the platform, some issues began to appear: there were very few controls regarding the quality of the extension and anyone was able to publish an extension, which may not work. So, Magento decided to create a new Magento Connect especially for Magento 2, which will be called the Magento Marketplace.

The end of the existing Connect website

By the time you read these lines, the existing Connect website will most probably still be available due to a number of reasons. Because all the Magento websites cannot be migrated in such a short period, clients still have some need for functionalities. Plus, many editors of extensions work exclusively on Magento extensions, so closing Connect can be dangerous for their business.

Finally, Magento wants to include Magento 1.x extensions in the new Magento Marketplace. In this way, a migration period has begun. The extensions have to pass through the new validation process, which I will introduce later. Connect will be discontinued a few months after the full launch of Marketplace.

A new business model

The important news that comes with the Magento Marketplace is that Magento has introduced a new revenue share business model. All the Magento Marketplace sales are subject to a 70/30 revenue share split with 70% of the revenue for the provider and 30% for Magento.

This changes every business model and you should take it into account when you decide to sell an extension.

Magento also explains that sales subject to the revenue share include both paid extensions and converted indirect leads from the **software as a service (SaaS)** or subscription-based products, such as a free extension bundled with a paid subscription. All the product/service bundles are subject to the same 70/30 revenue share business model.

A specific submission workflow

As I explained in the introduction, Magento Marketplace has to provide the best extensions for Magento in order to ensure that the solution represents a high level of integrators and stores. In this way, a strict process line has to be respected with the objective distribution in the marketplace.

The Magento Extension Distribution and Service Agreement

To participate in the Magento Marketplace, all developers must agree to the terms outlined in the Magento Extension Distribution and Service Agreement. I will summarize the main part of it.

Coding standards

Magento wants to ensure that developers who publish their extensions on the Marketplace are not plagiarizers and respect the Magento coding standards. This includes that the functionality has to be useful and not contain any hidden code.

Coding standards concern PHP first, but also your JavaScript and HTML code too.

 Read the full coding standards on this page: `http://devdocs.magento.com/guides/v2.0/coding-standards/bk-coding-standards.html`.

Branding

Magento has insisted for a long time on its registered trademark; it means that you cannot use the Magento word as you want.

For example, your extension's name can't contain `a Magento extension` in order to be sure that you don't suggest an affiliation with Magento. Be sure not to use the word `Magento` in your extension icon, domain name, username, or e-mail.

 I recommend you to get full information about using the trademark here: `http://docs.magento.com/marketplace/user_guide/getting-started/guidelines.html`.

Pricing and licensing

Your extension can still be offered for free. If you want to sell it, you will be able to choose the price, which will be in US dollars.

In any case, your product has to be handled by terms of use, which can be one of the most popular licenses (OSL-3.0, AFL, BSD-2 ...) or even a custom license.

Packaging and submitting the extension

We have seen how to package an extension with the composer in *Chapter 1, Introduction to Extension Development*. This is the first and only way to distribute your extension on Magento Marketplace.

Next, you'll have to zip it. Just execute the following command to do so:

```
zip -r ticketblaster.zip [EXTENTION_PATH]
```

In order to publish your extension, you must perform the following steps:

1. Create an account on Magento Marketplace as a developer at the following URL: `https://www.magentocommerce.com/magento-connect/customer/account/create/`.

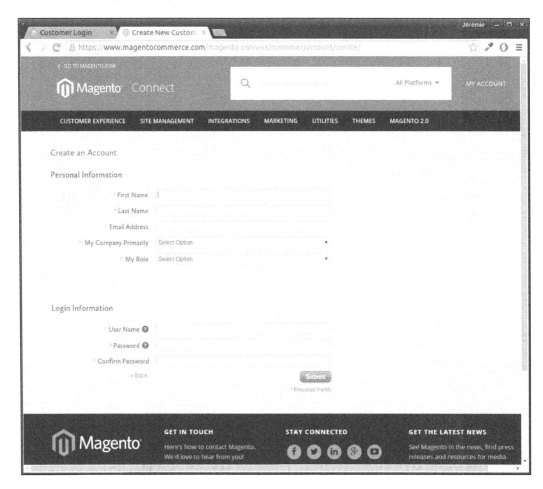

2. Go to the **My products** page and click on **Extensions** and then **Add Extension**.

3. You have to inform Magento about the compatibility version of your extension and if your extension offers additional services. Select the proper option and then click on **Continue**.

4. Enter the extension title and the public version number. Then, upload the ZIP file previously created.

The extension will automatically enter in the following step: the technical review.

The product profile

Once the extension is uploaded, a product profile will be created. On this page you can describe the extension with:

- Short and long descriptions
- Images
- YouTube videos
- Categories
- Version compatibility
- Supported browsers
- Languages used by the extension

You can add license types, stability settings, release notes, and finally, the pricing information. The page displays other information, such as the review statuses, which we will see in the following pages.

> Magento proposes **Messaging**, a new system used for communication between the developer and the Marketplace team regarding the extension.

Your personal and company profiles

Your company profile and your personal profile are similar; they provide the information about your company that appears on your Magento Marketplace listing.

You are able to complete the following:

- Your company's name
- Your company's bio and logo
- Your company's website

Technical review

This process begins when you upload the extension.

During the technical review, each package component is validated. The first part of the technical review is an automated process that can take up to 24 hours to complete. The code is analyzed to ensure that it meets our coding standards, is checked for malware, and scanned for evidence of plagiarism.

When the automated scan is complete, the Marketplace Administrator reviews the submission. If everything is in order, the status changes to **Ready for Marketing Review**.

If an extension fails to pass the technical review, you can correct the problems and resubmit the extension.

 You can read the complete code validation rules here:
http://docs.magento.com/marketplace/user_
guide/extensions/review-code-validation.html.

Here are the three statuses your extension can have after the technical review:

- **Ready for Marketing Review**: If your extension passes the technical review, the status will change to **Ready for Marketing Review**. You will receive an e-mail notifying you that the product has passed the technical review, and you can begin to work on the profile in preparation for the marketing review.

- **Ready for Use**: If a shared package passes the technical review, the status will change to **Ready for Use**. You will receive an e-mail notifying you that your shared package is approved, and it will become immediately available to be included with the other extensions that you submit.

- **Requires Developer Action**: If a submission is rejected during the technical review, the status will change to **Requires Developer Action**, and an e-mail will be sent notifying the change. You are welcome to correct the problem and resubmit the extension.

Marketing review

Magento doesn't explain how the marketing review will be managed, but we can guess that all the information you use for the presentation of your extension will be analyzed with respect to their branding rules.

You can read the full branding guidelines at `http://docs.magento.com/marketplace/user_guide/getting-started/guidelines.html`.

Selling extensions by ourselves

We have seen that Magento Marketplace sales are subject to a 70/30 revenue share split. This is only a matter of the sales that are made through the Marketplace. This means that you can sell your extension by yourself and keep the entire revenue.

The downloadable product

The best Magento product type destined to sell extensions is the downloadable product. Thanks to this product type, your extension can be sold easily.

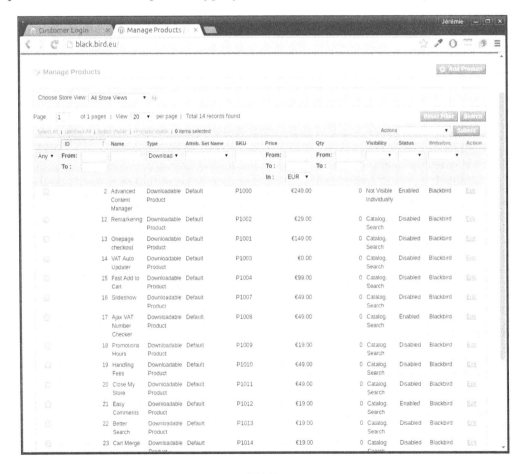

Managing versions with downloadable information

I recommend you to lend to your customers a version history: they will be able to download the exact version they need when they install or update its website. At the same time, showing all the versions will be a useful shop window for informing your customers that the extensions are live and are maintained!

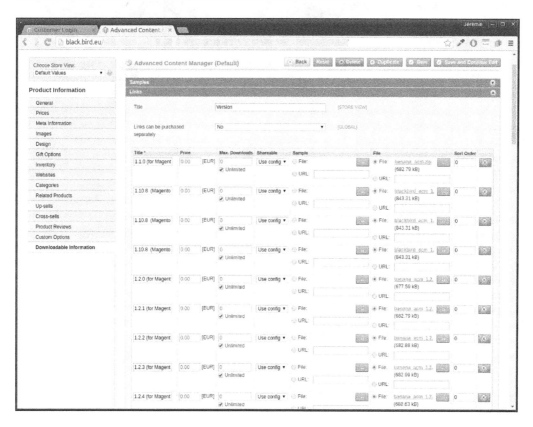

Selling additional services

The second important point to propose is additional services, such as the installation service or an extension of the support period. Use **Custom Options** to make the following:

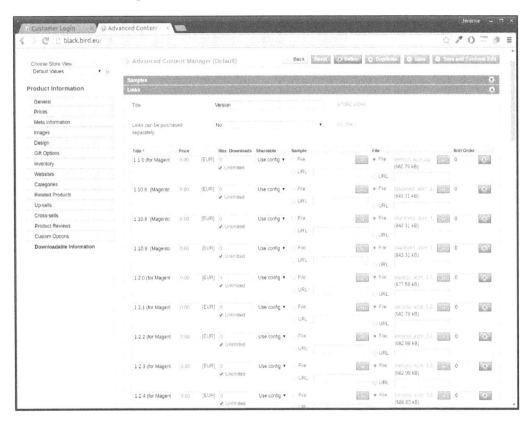

Having a store is not enough

You are the best person to know this: having an online store is not enough to begin selling your extension by yourself. You'll have to develop the frontend, configure at least one payment method (such as PayPal), and organize the SEO.

The potential success of your online store is exactly the same as one of your customer's shops: you have to be serious, engaged, and professional to propose a high-quality relationship during the customer's experience.

Summary

In this last chapter, we discovered how to sell your extension and propose to your customers the best approach to be fully reliable and trustworthy. Finally, by reading this book, you have all the keys to learn everything that is needed to become an invaluable extension editor, whether it is for your customers needs or for your own requirements.

I hope you discovered how Magento offers us a fantastic playground to develop everything you need in order to make the e-commerce innovative and secure.

Index